THE RABBIT BOOK
A Guide to Raising and Showing Rabbits

Text by Samantha Johnson
Photography by Daniel Johnson

VOYAGEUR
PRESS

Quarto is the authority on a wide range of topics.

Quarto educates, entertains and enriches the lives of our readers—enthusiasts and lovers of hands-on living.

www.quartoknows.com

First published in 2011 by Voyageur Press, an imprint of Quarto Publishing Group USA Inc., 400 First Avenue North, Suite 400, Minneapolis, MN 55401 USA. Telephone: (612) 344-8100 Fax: (612) 344-8692

quartoknows.com
Visit our blogs at quartoknows.com

Voyageur Press titles are also available at discounts in bulk quantity for industrial or sales-promotional use. For details write to Special Sales Manager at Quarto Publishing Group USA Inc., 400 First Avenue North, Suite 400, Minneapolis, MN 55401 USA.

Library of Congress Cataloging-in-Publication Data
Johnson, Samantha.
 The rabbit book : a guide to raising and showing rabbits / text, Samantha Johnson ; photography, Daniel Johnson.
    p. cm.
 Includes bibliographical references and index.
 ISBN 978-0-7603-3947-3 (flexibound)
 1. Rabbits. I. Johnson, Daniel, 1984- II. Title.
 SF453.J527 2010
 636.932'2--dc22
                          2010016325

Editors: Danielle Ibister and Melinda Keefe
Design Managers: Katie Sonmor and LeAnn Kuhlmann
Series designed by Pauline Molinari
Layout by Erin Fahringer

Printed in USA

Contents

Acknowledgments

I would like to thank the following people who were particularly helpful during the process of writing this book. I could not have done it by myself!

- My editor, Danielle Ibister, for all of her help and support! Thanks also to everyone at Voyageur Press for the opportunity to work on this project—thank you!
- Lorin, Paulette, Em, Anna, and J. Keeler for devoting many hours to proofreading and for offering lots of great suggestions.
- Dan—for the wonderful photos and for snapping my author bio photo, even though it "doesn't look like me."
- Cadi—of course.
- Tessa, Pierre, and Louie—models extraordinaire.

In memory of two very special rabbits:
Bonnie and Sofie

Welcome to Raising Rabbits

I was in 4-H "forever," as I'm sure many of you have been as well. Over the years, I was involved with many project areas, but rabbits were always one of my favorites. Although my first childhood rabbits were large mixed breeds—therefore ineligible for showing at my county fair—I still enjoyed them very much. Later I got started with purebred Netherland Dwarf rabbits, and then added Dutch and Holland Lops. In between I've also dabbled in the Rex and Jersey Wooly breeds.

But enough about me—how about you? What is your rabbit story? Whether you've just started with rabbits or have raised them for a while, you will find lots of helpful information in this book to guide you on your way.

Parts of a Rabbit

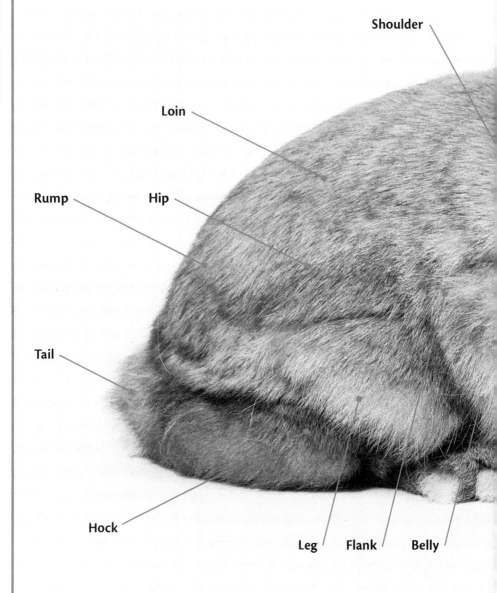

Shoulder

Loin

Rump

Hip

Tail

Hock

Leg

Flank

Belly

6

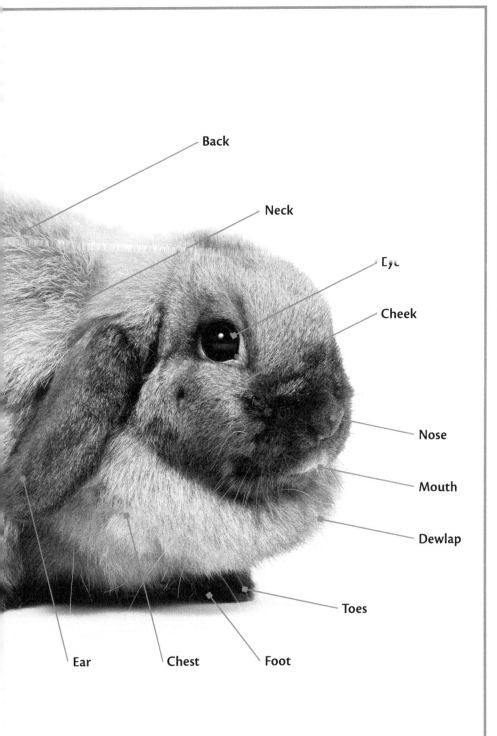

Back

Neck

Eye

Cheek

Nose

Mouth

Dewlap

Toes

Ear

Chest

Foot

Getting Started with Rabbits

With all of the breeds and varieties to choose from, you might feel a little bewildered when you think about selecting just one or two breeds to focus on in your rabbit project. The best thing to do is to research ahead of time, studying the different breeds and their characteristics. In this chapter, we'll discuss breeds, colors, shapes, and fur types.

If you're going to be raising purebred rabbits, then it is usually recommended that you begin with a trio of rabbits of a single breed (more on this in Chapter 3). If you're not in a hurry to begin breeding bunnies of your own, then I would recommend beginning with three or four rabbits of different breeds and sizes. It's easy to read about the differences between a five-pound rabbit and a ten-pound rabbit, or the differences between a Rex coat and an Angora coat, but nothing compares to the actual day-to-day aspects of caring for rabbits of different breeds. Then, after you've decided upon the breeds that suit you best, you can sell or trade the other rabbits that don't suit you.

I have owned many different breeds of rabbits over the years, but I only keep three breeds in my rabbitry at the moment. Why? Because after working with some of the breeds, I decided that they just weren't right for me. I admire the beauty of the Angora breeds, but they require more intensive grooming than I have time for, so I no longer keep any wooly breeds. After years with large (eight- to nine-pound) rabbits, I've downsized and now keep only the smaller breeds. This is what works for me; you'll

What's right for you? When selecting a breed of rabbit, always take your time and thoroughly consider your options.

All domestic rabbit breeds are descended from a particular variety of European rabbit (*Oryctolagus cuniculus*) although there are many types of wild rabbit, including this Eastern Cottontail.

want to experiment until you find the breeds that suit you best. You might love large breeds, or you might love Rex fur, or you might love lop ears, or you might love spots.

For rabbit show enthusiasts, smaller breeds such as the Holland Lop, the Mini Rex, and the Netherland Dwarf are immensely popular.

Extremely popular as show rabbits, Mini Rex are endearing for their size, disposition, and Rex fur.

Popular with adult and youth exhibitors alike, the Holland Lop is a fun combination of lop ears and a sweet temperament in a dwarf-sized package.

Popular Breeds

This subject is a bit tricky, as popularity varies depending on the criteria. For commercial rabbit breeders who raise rabbits for meat, New Zealand White, Californian, and Florida White rabbits are by far the most popular. For fiber art enthusiasts, the Angora breeds are the peak of perfection. For rabbit show enthusiasts, smaller breeds such as the Holland Lop, the Mini Rex, and the Netherland Dwarf are immensely popular.

Generally speaking, the smaller breeds are gaining in popularity, especially if you consider the fact that nine of the ten most recently developed rabbit breeds weigh less than six pounds. Many people enjoy the fact that smaller rabbits are easier to handle and manage. Small breeds also require less hutch space and produce less manure. On the other hand, many people love raising large (and giant!) rabbits, so it really does come down to personal preference, and what your goals are for your rabbit project. If you're raising rabbits for a meat pen project, then you'll probably want to consider one of the more popular commercial breeds. If raising show rabbits catches your fancy, then you might opt for one of the dwarf breeds—a Netherland Dwarf perhaps, or a Polish.

The Lionhead is not yet officially recognized by the ARBA but maintains many devoted fans.

Developing New Breeds

There are many rabbit breeds that are not yet recognized by the American Rabbit Breeders Association (ARBA), some of which are currently in varying stages of the ARBA's Certificate of Development program. The **Lionhead** is a small rabbit that boasts the unusual characteristic of a wooly mane around its neck, and the **Velveteen Lop** is an interesting composite of Rex fur with the long, lopped ears of an English Lop.

Additionally, the **Brazilian** is currently gaining a lot of attention, and there are also a handful of **Perlfee** rabbits in the United States. These two breeds are still many years away from ARBA recognition, but the Lionheads and Velveteen Lops are closer to becoming recognized breeds.

Heritage Breeds

Eleven heritage rabbit breeds are considered either rare or endangered, and these breeds are listed on the conservation priority list of the American Livestock Breeds Conservancy (ALBC). These breeds have a global population of fewer than two thousand or, in some cases, fewer than five hundred. Many rabbit breeders are expanding their rabbitries to include at least one of these heritage breeds, in hopes of increasing the population (and popularity!) to assure the breed's continuation. These breeds are:

American
American Chinchilla
Belgian Hare
Beveren
Crème d'Argent
Giant Chinchilla
Hotot
Lilac
Rhinelander
Silver
Silver Fox

All of these breeds are on the larger end of the weight scale, which makes sense when you consider that today's most popular rabbit breeds are under six pounds. It is interesting to consider that two of the breeds on the conservation priority list (the American Chinchilla and the Belgian Hare) were vastly popular in the early twentieth century with populations in the tens of thousands.

Raising heritage breeds can be a challenging pursuit, although a rewarding

There is a great deal of renewed interest in the heritage rabbit breeds, including the critically rare Silver Fox.

and satisfactory one as well. Many breeders have expressed concern over the difficulty in obtaining quality breeding stock. When a breed is rare, it's not likely that you'll find an abundance of animals for sale in your area. Chances are, you're not going to open up your local newspaper and see an ad for "Rare American Sable Rabbits for Sale." (But if you did, you would be very fortunate!) If you're serious about raising a rare breed, you'll want to locate a breeder of quality stock and then work on making travel arrangements for the rabbits. This may involve a road trip or shipping the rabbits by air. Some people offer transportation service for rabbits to and from major shows, so you could have someone pick up a rabbit for you at a show and transport it to you.

Colors, Colors, Colors

As you begin to browse the different rabbit breeds, you will notice that some are found in only one color. This is the breed's "standard" color. Examples are the Chinchilla breeds (the American Chinchilla, the Standard Chinchilla, and the Giant Chinchilla), the Florida

Blue—the color of this American Fuzzy Lop—is produced through the actions of a recessive gene. Some rabbits are carriers of the blue (dilute) gene even though they themselves do not exhibit the color. If you breed two black rabbits and they produce a blue kit, you'll know that both parents carry a copy of the blue (dilute) gene.

WHAT'S "BROKEN", AND SHOULD I FIX IT?

This is a very good question. In rabbits, a coat that comprises a dark color intermixed with white is known as a broken pattern. There are several breeds that exhibit the broken color pattern, including: the American Fuzzy Lop, French Angora, Checkered Giant, Dutch, English Spot, Jersey Wooly, English Lop, French Lop, Holland Lop, Mini Lop, Netherland Dwarf, Polish, Rex, Mini Rex, Rhinelander, Satin, New Zealand, and Havana.

You should always remember that the base color (the solid color) of a broken-patterned rabbit must be one of the base colors recognized in that particular breed. For instance, you wouldn't want to buy a broken Lilac Polish rabbit as a show prospect, since Lilac is not a recognized color in the Polish breed.

It is also helpful to understand a bit of the genetics behind the production of broken-patterned rabbits. A broken rabbit must have at least one broken-patterned parent. The broken pattern is a dominant gene that does not skip generations. Therefore, if you breed a broken buck to a solid doe, your odds of producing broken-patterned offspring are 50/50. If you breed a solid buck to a solid doe, your odds of producing broken-patterned offspring are zero.

But what happens when you breed a broken buck to a broken doe? Will it result in 100 percent broken kits? Not necessarily. Odds are that approximately 25 percent of the kits will still be solids, unless either of the parents is homozygous for the broken pattern (meaning that they carry two copies of the broken gene). These homozygous rabbits are known as "Charlies." Charlies typically display considerably more white than a rabbit with only one copy of the broken pattern, and as such, their markings usually do not fall within the necessary parameters outlined in the ARBA's *Standard of Perfection*. For instance, broken-patterned rabbits are supposed to retain their solid-colored ears, the "butterfly" pattern on their nose, and solid color around their eyes. Charlies like to defy these rules and are often unshowable.

A Charlie can be useful for breeding, however, especially if crossed with a solid-colored rabbit. A Charlie crossed with a solid-colored rabbit will result in 100 percent broken kits, each carrying one copy of the broken gene. This increases their chances of exhibiting "proper" broken patterns with the necessary markings in the necessary places.

Additionally, bear in mind that some of the breeds with broken patterns have very specific guidelines as to their particular pattern of markings. These breeds include the Checkered Giant, the English Spot, the Rhinelander, and the Dutch. These breeds are renowned for their specific patterns, and animals must meet these standards in order to be successfully shown.

Keep a lookout for broken English Angoras in the future; they are currently in development!

Always purchase rabbits that display colors that are recognized for their breed. For instance, this black Japanese patterned Harlequin is very eye-catching, but this color pattern on a Netherland Dwarf would be unacceptable.

White, the American Sable, the Lilac, the Cinnamon, the Dwarf Hotot, the Silver, the Giant Angora, the Crème d'Argent, the Champagne d'Argent, the Californian, the Himalayan, the Silver Fox, the Silver Marten, the Tan, and several of the spotted breeds. If choosing a specific color and raising rabbits that exclusively exhibit that color appeals to you, then think seriously about choosing one of the above breeds.

On the other hand, if producing a rainbow of rabbit colors is your cup of tea, then you might want to consider a breed that is found in a multitude of colors: Holland Lops, for instance, or Netherland Dwarfs. The Rex and Mini Rex breeds are also found in myriad colors, as are some of the other small breeds, such as the American Fuzzy Lop and the Jersey Wooly.

One important thing to keep in mind regarding colors: you will want to make sure that you purchase rabbits in recognized colors. The ARBA only recognizes certain colors for each breed, but unrecognized colors do occur in litters from time to time. For instance, the rare American breed is only recognized in two colors: white and blue. This doesn't mean that every litter of American kits consists of entirely blues or whites. On the contrary, several different colors are frequently seen, including reds. You wouldn't want to make the mistake of purchasing a red American as a show prospect, only to discover later that your rabbit is an unrecognized color. Do your homework first, and learn the accepted colors of any breeds that you're considering.

DWARF BREEDS: TAKING A WALK ON THE WILD SIDE?

You may have heard people discouraging youth breeders from working with dwarf rabbit breeds. The reason? Dwarf breeds have a reputation for being high-strung and difficult to handle. This could be said of rabbits of any breed in certain circumstances—but is it particularly true of dwarf breeds?

The answer depends on whom you ask. I have owned Netherland Dwarfs for many years and have not noticed them to be distinctly different from my larger breeds. In fact, the Netherland Dwarfs I have known are outgoing and enjoy attention. Now, you could ask another person with different experiences and receive a completely different response. Britannia Petites, in particular, are noted as being "show rabbits" that are unsuitable for young rabbit enthusiasts.

The bottom line? Ask a breeder. If you're considering a particular dwarf breed and are going to a rabbitry to take a look, go ahead and ask if the breed is suitable for a youth exhibitor. Most breeders don't want to sell a rabbit into a situation where the buyer may end up unhappy, so if they feel that their breed wouldn't be appropriate for you, they will likely say so.

Another option would be to ask friends who keep dwarf breeds if you can spend some time interacting with their rabbits. Get a feel for their dispositions, temperaments, and general character. Some time spent handling a dwarf rabbit may answer your questions about their high-strung reputation.

Dwarf rabbits, such as the Netherland Dwarf, are popular as show rabbits.

SHAPES

The ARBA classifies the forty-seven recognized rabbit breeds into five different shapes. It's important to understand the differences, as each breed is posed on the show table mainly according to its shape. Let's take a look at the five shapes and the breeds that exhibit them. (For full descriptions of the characteristics of each shape, please see my previous book, *The Field Guide to Rabbits*.)

Compact

- American Fuzzy Lop
- English Angora
- Dutch
- Dwarf Hotot
- Florida White
- Havana
- Holland Lop*
- Jersey Wooly
- Lilac
- Mini Lop
- Mini Rex
- Netherland Dwarf*
- Polish
- Silver
- Standard Chinchilla
- Thrianta

A Dwarf Hotot is an example of the *compact* shape.

*Holland Lops and Netherland Dwarfs are posed in a slightly different fashion than the typical compact-shaped rabbit. Refer to ARBA's *Standard of Perfection* for specific information on how each breed should be posed on the show table.

Commercial

- American Chinchilla
- American Sable
- Californian
- Champagne d'Argent
- Cinnamon
- Crème d'Argent
- French Angora
- French Lop
- Giant Angora
- Harlequin
- Hotot
- Mini Satin
- New Zealand
- Palomino
- Rex
- Satin
- Satin Angora
- Silver Fox
- Silver Marten

A Californian is an example of the *commercial* shape.

Semi-Arch

- American
- Beveren
- English Lop
- Flemish Giant
- Giant Chinchilla

An English Lop is an example of the *semi-arch* shape.

Full Arch

- Belgian Hare
- Britannia Petite
- Checkered Giant
- English Spot
- Rhinelander
- Tan

A Britannia Petite is an example of the *full arch* shape.

Cylindrical

- Himalayan

And, yes, a Himalayan is the only breed that exhibits the *cylindrical* shape.

Fur Types

Another aspect to consider is fur—what type will best suit your needs for your rabbit program? There are four fur types: normal fur, Satin fur, Rex fur, and Angora wool. Let's explore each type.

Normal fur

Normal fur is the average bunny fur, and is found on thirty-seven of the forty-seven rabbit breeds recognized by the ARBA. Normal fur is exactly as its name implies: basic bunny hair, unembellished by anything extraordinary. Normal fur is subdivided into two types, however: fly back and roll back.

> Fly back coats are aptly named, as they "fly back" into their original position after you run your hand along the fur in the opposite direction. Roll backs, on the other hand, stay "roughed up" without falling back into position.

Fly back coats are aptly named, as they "fly back" into their original position after you run your hand along the fur in the opposite direction. Roll backs, on the other hand, stay "roughed up" without falling back into position.

The Holland Lop, like most breeds, displays what is known as "normal" fur. It is not long and impressive like the Angora, it lacks the velvet-like density of the Rex coat, and it does not have the transparent sheen of the Satin coat.

An impressive sight! A quality Rex rabbit with an impeccable coat exhibits the thick and dense softness for which the breed is renowned.

Rex fur

Rex fur is renowned for its softness and dense quality. It is short, approximately ⅝ inch, and the coarse guard hairs do not protrude. This allows for the extreme density and softness of the Rex coat. Rex fur is found in the Rex breed (how did you guess?), as well as in the Mini Rex. The Velveteen Lop (currently in development and not yet officially recognized by the ARBA) also features Rex fur.

Satin fur

This unique fur is like no other! The Satin coat was originally discovered in the 1930s and is believed to have originated as a genetic mutation in the Havana breed. Satin fur is noted for its transparent sheen and the glasslike appearance of the hair shafts. Satin fur is found in three breeds: the Satin, the Mini Satin, and the Satin Angora.

Satin fur—seen in the Satin (shown here) and Mini Satin breeds—is remarkable for its transparent luster.

Angora wool, anyone? The sheer magnitude of the English Angora's coat makes the breed hard to overlook, but the daily grooming commitment is extensive.

The Jersey Wooly provides Angora wool in a petite package. Jersey Woolys are a wonderful choice if you'd like to get acquainted with raising Angora rabbits on a small scale.

Angora wool

Angora wool is the fiber enthusiast's paradise! If you're familiar with Angora goats or Angora sheep, you'll easily recognize the long, soft, flowing wool that Angora rabbits possess.

There are six rabbit breeds that exhibit Angora wool. These include two dwarf-sized breeds (the American Fuzzy Lop and the Jersey Wooly), and four larger breeds (the English Angora, the French Angora, the Satin Angora, and the Giant Angora). All of these breeds are found in a multitude of colors, with the exception of the Giant Angora, which is only found in Ruby-Eyed White. If you're looking for a rabbit breed with fur that is easy to care for, then the Angora breeds should probably not be first on your list. However, if you enjoy grooming and are up to the challenge and commitment of daily care and attention, you'll undoubtedly find that raising Angora breeds is a rewarding and fulfilling experience.

The Belgian Hare, now quite rare, is one of only six breeds that exhibit the full arch shape.

I Want to Try Them All!

It's a perfectly natural reaction. You're just beginning your rabbit project. You've read books, talked to friends, and visited a couple of shows. You've seen Mini Lops, Rex, Satins, Angoras, and Dwarf Hotots. You've been reading about heritage rabbit breeds and would love to help preserve a rare breed.

As tempting as it might be to raise ten or twelve or twenty different breeds, you really want to keep yourself more restricted.

Choose two or three breeds that *really* catch your fancy, and begin with those. You don't need to have breeding trios for all of them right now; just one or two rabbits per breed will suffice. This allows you to get acquainted with the breed without overburdening yourself. Always be sure that you keep your rabbitry to a manageable size and don't spread yourself too thin. As cute as they are, each rabbit you keep will need individualized care and attention.

Making breed choices can be difficult. You might like the coat pattern of the Dutch, the velvety fur of the Rex, or the lopped ears of the Mini Lop and may have a difficult time narrowing yourself to only one or two breeds.

Whether you choose a popular breed or an unusual one, take care to select only the very best animals for breeding or show.

CHAPTER 2

Setting Up Your Rabbitry

In This Section

Raising rabbits is a commitment to be taken seriously. Your rabbits depend on you each and every day for their food, water, and care. This is important to keep in mind as you establish your rabbit project. You are committing to a daily responsibility that can't be ignored when it isn't convenient. Rain or snow, in sickness and in health, your rabbits need you and your attention.

Before you acquire any rabbits, make sure that you have a family member or friend who will be able to care for your rabbits whenever you need a helping hand.

Before you bring home your first cute and cuddly rabbit friend, be sure that you have everything prepared in advance, including hutches, feeders, and waterers.

Keep an eye on your rabbits. Daily observation is an important part of keeping your rabbits happy and healthy.

If you're going away for the weekend or off to a rabbit show, someone will need to tend to any rabbits left at home.

It's best if you establish a daily schedule and stick to it as closely as possible. This is beneficial to you as well as your rabbits. They are creatures of habit and thrive on a schedule. For instance, you might feed your bunnies their hay and pellets each morning at 7:00 a.m. You could theoretically leave it at that, but I strongly recommend a second feeding for your rabbits at night. Do a nightly check at 7:00 p.m; hand out another small feeding of pellets and some additional hay. At both

of these feedings, check each rabbit's water and refill as necessary. You'll also be checking to see that each rabbit is happy, alert, and hungry. You'll begin to learn each rabbit's personality and habits, and soon you'll be able to recognize what's normal for each rabbit and what might be cause for alarm.

Indoors or Out?

Will you be housing your rabbits inside a garage, barn, or shed? Or will you be keeping them out of doors in a sturdy hutch? There are merits to both methods of rabbit keeping, so let's explore each of them.

Indoors

A barn, garage, shed, or other outbuilding can be an excellent place to keep your rabbits. The benefits are many: your rabbits have protection from predators, they have shelter from inclement weather, and they are subject to fewer temperature fluctuations.

Ventilation is vital to a rabbit's health and well-being, so fresh air must be available to rabbits that are housed in a building. On the other hand, harsh breezes are not healthy for rabbits either. You'll want to maintain a balance: a regular turnover of fresh air throughout your rabbit building, while keeping the brunt of the breeze away from your bunnies.

Lighting can be helpful in increasing your does' breeding rates during the winter months. Artificial lighting mimics the longer days of spring and summer, thus increasing your chances of raising successful litters during the shorter days of fall and winter. By keeping your rabbits in a building, it's possible to provide additional lighting to artificially lengthen their days.

Lighting will be important for you as well; working in your rabbit building should be a positive and pleasant experience, and sufficient lighting will help to achieve this goal.

HOUSE RABBITS

There is a third option for rabbit keeping, and this is the "house rabbit" method. In this type of rabbit care, your rabbit is allowed to roam freely within your home. This requires litter training your rabbit (not hard to do, as they are predisposed to being tidy in this regard) and thoroughly rabbit-proofing any rooms in your house that your rabbit may have access to. Houseplants, electrical cords, and other pets may all prove harmful to your house rabbit, so think and plan carefully before taking this step.

Caution aside, it's absolutely certain that you'll have hours of fun as you watch your rabbit's antics and play in the comfort of your living room (see more on house rabbits in Chapter 8).

Rabbit-proofing is an important consideration for a house rabbit. Electrical cords, house plants, and other potential dangers may lurk.

This small rabbitry is indoors, and the cages are protected from all types of inclement weather.

Outdoors

Rabbits kept outdoors will need a hutch or a reinforced cage that is strong enough to protect them from predators. Generally speaking, hutches have wooden portions, while cages are all-wire. A hutch is the sturdiest and safest housing option for outdoor rabbits. If you want to use cages for outdoor use, you will need to reinforce the edges with wood or build the cages up on wooden platforms to keep them out of harm's way.

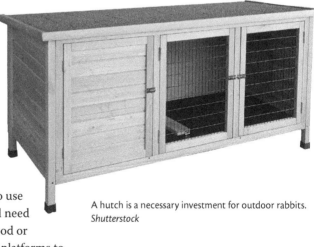

A hutch is a necessary investment for outdoor rabbits. *Shutterstock*

Obviously, rabbits kept outdoors have continual access to optimal ventilation; however, take care to place your hutches in a shaded location that

29

These outdoor hutches have solid ceilings to keep out rain and wire mesh to keep bunnies in and predators out.

is out of direct sunlight. Never place a rabbit's cage in direct sunlight, either outdoors or in front of a sunny window. Rabbits do not handle heat well and succumb to heat stroke easily. Don't make the mistake of giving your bunnies access to much sunshine; they'll thank you for the shade.

If you live in a cold climate with harsh winters, you will find yourself dealing with frozen water crocks or bottles. Fresh water is one of your foremost priorities in rabbit care, and you will need to provide it regularly. Plastic water bottles are prone to cracking in cold weather; use water cups or crocks to avoid this problem. Your rabbits will need their frozen water removed and refreshed at least twice per day; three times is better. This problem makes the case for keeping rabbits indoors; the warmer temperatures inside a barn or shed may make the difference between dealing with frozen water or not.

> Never place a rabbit's cage in direct sunlight, either outdoors or in front of a sunny window. Rabbits do not handle heat well and succumb to heat stroke easily.

This outdoor hutch is shaded by the trees, which is always a sensible idea.

IS IT LEGAL?

Before you make any rabbit purchases, investigate your local city ordinances. Some ordinances restrict you from keeping livestock such as rabbits on your property, especially if you live in an urban area. Other ordinances may allow rabbits but may place limitations on the number of rabbits that you can keep. In most areas, it's perfectly fine to keep rabbits, it's just something that you should verify before bringing any bunnies home.

Hutches and Cages

As mentioned, a rabbit hutch is made of wood and wire; this is the best housing method for outdoor rabbits. A rabbit cage is a much simpler, all-wire enclosure; it is less sturdy and more prone to breakage but perfectly appropriate for indoor use.

There are a few different options for purchasing cages. You can find rabbit cage kits at your local Tractor Supply Company store or similar establishments, and you can purchase them online from farm supply stores. Additionally, there are many companies that provide rabbit

equipment exclusively, and these can be excellent sources for obtaining housing for your rabbits. Many of these companies have their catalog listings online, so a quick Internet search of "rabbit equipment suppliers" should provide you with plenty of sources to start with. You may find it easier to request their print catalogs in order to view their product inventory more easily. (These catalogs are valuable to have on hand, since most equipment suppliers also sell all manner of rabbit supplies, including medical products, feeders, and grooming tools. You will undoubtedly find

A large wooden hutch can provide ample space for weaning a litter of baby rabbits.

This rabbit is housed in a cage that is made of hard plastic. It is easy to clean and more aesthetically pleasing than wire mesh. The downside? Plastic can be chewed by rabbits, unlike wire mesh. A cage of this type would also be unsuitable for use outdoors.

many products that will be helpful to your rabbit project.)

You might feel a little overwhelmed when you view the options for cages and hutches. There is a vast array of sizes, including 18×24 inches, 24×24 inches, 24×36 inches, 30×36 inches, and many others—and all of these come in a wide range of styles and types. How do you know which will be best for your needs?

The size of the cage or hutch you buy depends on the size of the rabbits you will be raising. If you're looking to get started with small rabbit breeds that weigh less than six pounds, then 24×24-inch housing is usually sufficient. Medium-sized rabbits weighing between six and ten pounds should have larger cages or hutches in the 30×36-inch range. Large and giant breeds weighing more than ten pounds will need plenty of extra room to move around; choose larger enclosures for these breeds. Also remember, if you have ample space, go ahead and select larger cages, regardless of the size of your bunnies; they'll appreciate the extra room to play.

You can also find rabbit cages that are entirely made of plastic—these are easy to assemble and rather cute, although they may not hold up as well over long-term use, due to the fact that rabbits might enjoy chewing the plastic.

Regardless of whether you select hutches or cages, you want to make sure that they are raised and the flooring is made of wire, so that the rabbit's droppings and urine can fall through to the ground (if kept outside) or into a tray underneath (definitely a must if the hutches are kept indoors, and you may still want to use a tray outdoors as well). If your enclosures have solid bottoms, the manure cannot fall through and your rabbit will end up sitting in the dirty area of his cage. This can cause medical problems such as hutch burn. You should provide floor mats or resting boards for your rabbit; these can be purchased from rabbit equipment suppliers. Resting boards give your rabbit a comfortable place to rest, while still allowing the droppings to fall through the wire floor in the other portions of the cage.

How Many Holes?

Rabbit enthusiasts use the word "holes" to describe the number of cages or hutches

in their rabbitry. Therefore, you may decide to have an "eight-hole rabbitry," with eight hutches, or you may decide to go with a "twelve-hole rabbitry," with twelve hutches and so on.

So how many holes do you need? The answer depends on how many rabbits you are planning to keep. You want at least one hole per rabbit, plus a couple of extra. You're always going to want to have more cages than you have rabbits. If you have eight holes, then you should aim for an average of six rabbits. The extra cage space gives you a place to keep your newly weaned rabbits.

To Tray, or Not To Tray?

If you keep your hutches outdoors, it's an option to allow the droppings and bits of hay and feed to fall through the floor directly to the ground. You can then rake up the waste. You can also make compost directly under the cages, or begin earthworm farming.

However, for many reasons, you may decide that you would rather not have the droppings falling on the ground; this is obviously true if you are keeping your rabbits in a building! In this case, you will want to have your cages or hutches equipped with removable trays.

Removable trays (also called "pans") are made of galvanized metal or plastic. Some rabbit breeders prefer the metal trays; I've tried both varieties and have switched all of my cages to plastic trays. To me, they are easier to handle (they're lighter!) and easier to clean. The plastic trays easily slide out, making cleaning time a snap.

Some breeders like to sprinkle pine shavings in the bottom of each tray for odor control; other breeders feel that the added shavings simply make cleaning

Many pre-built cages and hutches are equipped with removable plastic trays, making cage-cleaning a snap.

more difficult. Another odor-reducing tip: sprinkle a small amount of baking soda in each tray after you clean it. The baking soda absorbs odors and helps to keep your rabbitry smelling fresh and clean.

Making Your Own Cages

While it's certainly very simple to purchase a rabbit cage kit or prefabricated rabbit cages from an equipment supplier, it's also possible to create your own rabbit cages from scratch. This is the least expensive route, but it does require being handy with tools.

Again, rabbit equipment suppliers come to your rescue, as some companies (Klubertanz Equipment Company is one) sell all of the components needed

to make rabbit cages. You can purchase rolls of wire mesh and welded wire, floor panels, cage doors, clips, rings, tools, and more. So if you're up to the challenge of working with raw materials (and have a willing assistant to give you a hand!), this might be the perfect opportunity to hone your craftsmanship skills and create the perfect dwelling for your future rabbits.

Wooden Hutch Kits

Hutch kits are considerably more expensive than cage kits, but they are deserving of mention, as they are a beautiful alternative to the traditional wire cage that is the average bunny abode. Today's wooden hutches can be extremely attractive and at the same time very practical for daily rabbit care. They typically have a floor that is half solid wood and half wire, giving your rabbit a comfortable place to sit while still allowing for the proper removal of droppings through the wire portion of the floor. If you can afford to invest in solid wooden hutches, they are certainly an excellent option. Wooden hutches are sturdy and offer extra protection against predators. Protection is absolutely necessary if you keep your rabbits outdoors.

Cleaning

It's sometimes surprising how quickly a rabbit building can become untidy, but you can stay ahead of the problem by sweeping the floors every day. This will eliminate the bits of loose hay and rabbit manure that gather around the outer edge of your hutches. A few minutes each day will prevent the job from building up into something bigger.

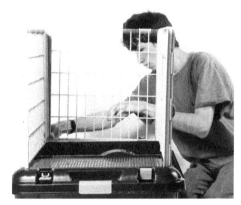

Your rabbit cages will also need to be regularly cleaned and the trays washed. Remove any old, loose hay and any bits of manure from the cage interior that didn't fall through the wire floor (this is usually done on a daily basis). You may also wish to thoroughly disinfect your cages a couple of times per year, or anytime that your rabbits have been ill. Simply move the rabbits to a safe location (a rabbit travel carrier works great for

Building a rabbit cage from a kit can be a fun and rewarding project. Always carefully look over all parts, tools, and instructions to be certain that everything is in order before you begin.

this, but large, sturdy cardboard boxes can suffice), and wash the cages or hutches with a bleach solution. Use one part bleach to sixteen parts water, then rinse with water.

Feeding and Watering

There are several options for getting food and water to your bunnies; you may decide to try a few different possibilities before you settle upon what works best for your situation.

One thing that's important to understand is that rabbits love to play with objects. Food and water bowls are fair game to an energetic rabbit. If the bowl is tipped over, the pellets or water spill through the wire floor and are completely wasted. You'll want to avoid this.

Feeders
- **Plastic snap-on cups, crocks, or feeders**: I like these, because they snap onto the wire of the cage wall and are not

Heavy-duty crocks can make good feeders for rabbits. They are heavy enough to prevent being easily tipped over.

easy for a busy bunny to spill. Plastic cups are also easy to clean and inexpensive. If your rabbit has figured out how to tip and spill the plastic cups or feeders, you can purchase "lock on" versions that should eliminate the problem.

- **Metal snap-on feeders**: Similar in shape and function to the plastic feeders, these are made of galvanized metal. Metal feeders are heavy-duty and not easy for bunnies to remove from the wire walls.
- **Heavy crocks**: These do not attach to the cage walls, but are heavy enough that they are not easy for a rabbit to tip over. These can be used for water as well.
- **Outside feeders** (sometimes known as J-feeders because of their shape) are one of the most popular types of feeder. An outside feeder made of galvanized steel attaches to the exterior of the cage wall. Then you cut an opening in the wire to allow room for the bottom portion of the feeder to extend inside the cage, while the upper portion of the feeder remains outside. This allows you to feed each rabbit its portion of pellets without opening each cage door. This can save time if you have a large rabbitry.

Bear in mind that not all outside feeders are created equal; there are variances that you will want to be aware of. Some have open tops, while others have flip-top lids that you must flip up in order to add the pellets. The flip-top lids are definitely the kind you want to have. This design keeps rodents and critters from climbing into your rabbit's cage via the feeder opening; it also helps to keep dust and debris from falling in the feeder. Some outside feeders have solid bottoms, while others have perforated bottoms. The type you choose will depend upon the type of pellets or feed that you're using. If you feed

supplemental seeds or any type of feed that is very tiny, you will want a solid-bottomed feeder to prevent the small bits from falling through. On the other hand, if you only feed traditional-sized pellets, then the feeders with perforated bottoms will likely work best. This will allow the pellet dust (called "fines") to fall through the holes, preventing the fines from collecting in the bottom of the feeder. Outside feeders can also be purchased in a plastic version, which I prefer. Sometimes the corners of the steel feeders can be very sharp, and although the feeders are usually safe, I have heard of incidences in which rabbits have been injured on steel outside feeders.

Waterers

- **Plastic snap-on cups or crocks**: Yes, the same ones that we previously discussed using as feeders can also be used as waterers. The same positive qualities exist when used as waterers: They are difficult for bunnies to remove from the cage wall, but easy for you to remove for cleaning. They are also quick to clean and inexpensive to buy.
- **Heavy crocks** also work well as water containers, as long as your rabbit leaves them alone and doesn't spill them regularly. You can experiment a bit to see if your rabbits behave themselves or not.
- **Water bottles**: These are a popular choice. They hold a large quantity of water, and they cannot be spilled. The water bottle attaches to the outside of the rabbit's cage, with the nozzle reaching inside the cage. The water is released when the rabbit licks the end of the nozzle, dislodging a metal ball, which allows the water to drip. When the rabbit stops licking the nozzle, the ball falls into place and the water stops dripping. This works well in theory

This steel feeder is an outside feeder. The lower portion is inserted into the cage (you'll have to cut the wire mesh to create an opening), while the rest of the feeder is mounted on the outside of the cage, allowing you to feed your rabbit without opening the cage door.

Feeders with perforated bottoms are great for reducing the build-up of "fines" (accumulated dust from pelleted feet), but they may not work well If you feed a grain mixture that is composed of very small bits. You may end up losing a significant amount of feed through the holes, as shown here.

No more spills! This type of plastic cup works very well as either a waterer or a feeder. The M-shaped piece is detachable, and you simply place the cup on the inside of your rabbit's cage with the M piece on the outside, with the wire in between. It works like a charm!

Water bottles are sometimes equipped with a piece of small plastic that floats, designed to let you easily see when your rabbit's water needs to be refilled.

and fairly well in real life; however, I have raised more than one rabbit that would not under any circumstances drink from a water bottle, despite repeated attempts to convince them otherwise. The moral here is to always make sure that your rabbit is using the water bottle before removing their other sources of water. Another thing to remember is that water bottles can be a bit more difficult to clean than water cups or crocks. You'll also want to watch out for any leakage problems.

- **Automatic watering systems** can be a good option if you have a large rabbitry. They aren't as practical if you have only a few rabbits. An automatic watering system provides continuous fresh water to all of your cages through a piping system. Very handy and efficient—but not as economical as the other options discussed.

Check at least twice per day to be sure that all water cups in your rabbitry are filled. Also check to make sure that pellets are available and that the hay racks are full. *Shutterstock*

Equipment

While you can certainly get by with cages, feeders, and waterers, there are a few other helpful pieces of equipment that you may wish to invest in.

Hay racks

Hay racks can be a helpful addition to your rabbitry equipment. They help to keep hay off the cage floor, which can reduce the amount wasted and lower your rabbit's risk of developing hutch burn (caused by sitting too long in soiled hay).

On the other hand, you may find that your rabbits do not consume as much hay when it's fed in a hay rack as they do when it's loose on the cage floor. Personally, my rabbits seem less inclined to munch on their hay when it isn't as easily accessible.

Certain types of hay racks allow for the hay bits to fall through to the floor, which can be messy and wasteful. Solid-backed hay racks can help to eliminate this problem. My advice would be to purchase a couple of solid-backed hay racks and give them a try. If you love them, invest in one for each of your rabbits; if you don't, you won't have invested much in a failed experiment.

Carriers

You're off to pick up your new rabbits—how will you transport them home? While a cardboard box could suffice, a rabbit carrier would be much better. Rabbit carriers are small, wire cages with attached trays underneath. Their flip-top lids allow for easy access and a safe ride for your long-eared friends. You can purchase carriers in single units, sets of two or three, or larger models. If you're just starting out with your rabbitry, a unit of two or three will probably be all you need.

Carriers are a must-have if you're planning to show your rabbits. Your

A hay rack is a great way to keep your rabbit's hay clean and dry. Hay racks are also helpful for keeping cages tidy.

While you can certainly transport rabbits in a travel carrier designed for a dog or a cat (*top*), a specially designed rabbit carrier (*bottom*) works even better! It has a wire mesh floor that allows droppings and urine to fall through to the tray underneath.

bunnies can happily travel with their food and water, while being in a safe environment the entire time.

Cage cart

If you're regularly showing lots of rabbits, you may find it cumbersome to haul around multiple carriers. To your rescue: the cage cart! Your carriers attach to a metal frame on wheels, making things easy as you haul your bunnies around the show facility.

Grooming stand

This is another must-have if you're planning to show regularly. A grooming stand or table is usually made of wood, with a soft, carpeted top where you can groom your rabbits with ease. These are sold in rabbit equipment catalogs.

Scale

This might not be something that you would think of immediately in terms of rabbit equipment needs, but a scale can be a helpful and valuable investment for your rabbitry. With a scale, you can easily monitor the growth of your young rabbits, you can evaluate whether your rabbits have achieved (or exceeded!) senior weight, and you can avoid showing rabbits that would be disqualified for being over- or underweight.

Scales that can be used to weigh small animals are available in a variety of types: digital scales, spring dial scales, hanging scales, or tabletop scales. They vary greatly in price and weight capacity, so if you're raising Flemish Giants, you wouldn't want to purchase a scale with a weight capacity

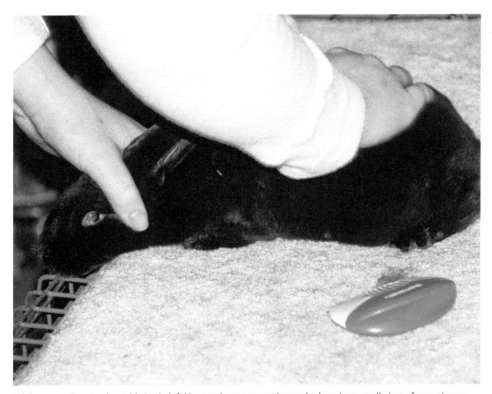

While a grooming stand or table is a helpful item to have, you can improvise by using a small piece of carpeting on which to groom your rabbits.

Purchasing a scale is a wise investment—you'll be able to closely monitor your rabbit's weight and rate of development.

of ten pounds. Explore the available options and make the wisest choice to fit your budget.

Floor mats

Also known as foot rests or resting boards, these plastic mats have openings to allow droppings to fall through, while still giving your rabbit a comfortable place to rest. These boards are particularly important for breeds that are more susceptible to developing sore hocks, such as Rex rabbits. You will want at least one floor mat for each cage—and you will probably want to add them to your carriers as well. Floor mats are relatively inexpensive (around three to seven dollars each) in comparison to the comfort and protection they provide for your rabbits. Plus, they are washable and easy to clean.

Fans

If you keep your rabbits indoors, it's vitally important that they have good ventilation and cool air. Enclosed buildings can become hot and stifling during the summer months if you're not careful. For these situations, fans are helpful. You can

SHOW CLASS DIVISIONS

Show rabbits are divided into classes by age and weight. The most common classes are **junior** (younger than six months) and **senior** (older than six months). Some shows also offer a **pre-junior** class for rabbits younger than three months. For large breeds that exceed nine pounds as adults, **intermediate** classes are offered for rabbits between six and eight months old. In each division, the show animal must meet the breed's weight requirements for that class. It is helpful to keep a small scale at home for this purpose.

purchase large, heavy-duty fans, or you can also find small individual cage fans to cool each rabbit's personal space.

Nest boxes

We'll discuss these in further detail in Chapter 7, as nest boxes are typically used for does and their litters. However, many rabbit enthusiasts like to provide nesting boxes to all of their rabbits. The nest box provides a "hidey-hole" for your rabbit and a quiet place to sleep and rest.

One note of caution: always pay attention to make sure that your rabbit is not using the nest box as a litter box. You wouldn't want to look in one day to see a nest box filled with droppings and wet hay.

Plastic floor mats or resting boards provide a comfortable place for your rabbit to rest off the wire floor.

Colony Raising

Generally speaking, rabbit-raising techniques have remained the same for many years, but some innovative rabbit raisers are returning to an "old-fashioned" type of rabbit management called the colony system.

Colony raising is the method of keeping multiple rabbits together in a large setting, reminiscent of the rabbit warrens that wild rabbits inhabit. Sometimes these colonies are established outdoors in large, fenced areas; other colonies are indoors, for instance in a large boxed stall with wooden sides and a dirt floor.

Colony raising allows rabbits more freedom in terms of exercise and digging, as well as access to vegetation

A nest box is essential for a doe with a litter. You may also want to provide nest boxes to your other rabbits for a place to sleep and rest.

Let's dig in! Colony raising provides your rabbits with the opportunity to live more naturally—digging and eating greens. But there are many considerations before embarking on this type of housing, including how to protect them from predators and keep them healthy.

Whenever your rabbit is outdoors, whether it's for exercise or because you're keeping him in a colony setting, you must keep watch vigilantly to be sure that your rabbit does not escape. Watch also for predators—both wild and domestic. Even the family dog can be of potential harm to your rabbits.

if the colony is outdoors. However, it can be considerably more difficult to manage each rabbit individually when they are kept in a colony setting. Illnesses can spread more rapidly when multiple rabbits are in regular close contact with one another. It can also be more difficult to ascertain the daily health of each rabbit when they are kept together. If one were to lose its appetite, you might not notice immediately, especially if all of the other rabbits are devouring the food.

Something else to keep in mind: people who have attempted colony raising have reported a higher incidence of loss in litters. To avoid this, some breeders choose to remove their pregnant does from the colony, opting instead to house the does and their subsequent litters in a hutch until the kits are weaned.

There are many considerations to ponder if you are planning an outdoor colony, as predators are a very real threat and not one to overlook. Fencing is of primary concern, largely to keep your

rabbits from escaping, but also to keep other animals from entering the colony. You can bury wire fencing underground to prevent animals from digging under the fence or extend hardware cloth or chicken wire over the entire top of the colony. In addition to threats from other mammals, birds and snakes also pose danger to your colony-raised rabbits, so take care to keep all of those species away from your rabbits at all times.

Handling Your Rabbits

You have two primary objectives when handling rabbits: (1) keep your rabbit safe and (2) don't get scratched.

Let's face it, it's not fun being scratched. Rabbits have exceptionally sharp little toenails, and having them dig into your arm isn't the most pleasant experience. It's recommended that you always wear a long-sleeved shirt when handling a rabbit. (For that matter, long pants are also advisable if your bunny will be sitting in your lap.)

SPECIAL SEASONAL CONSIDERATIONS

Shutterstock

Methods of rabbit keeping do vary a bit from season to season, and there are seasonal considerations to always keep in mind.

If you live in a climate with cold, wintry conditions, then you will be faced with the trial of keeping fresh water in front of your rabbits during frigid weather. Anyone who has tried it will sympathize with the frustrations of finding frozen water crocks or bottles on icy winter mornings. What then, to do?

If you have the option of keeping your rabbits inside a building during the winter months, this will certainly increase your chances of keeping their water thawed. If you have access to a building with heat (a garage heated to approximately 50 degrees Fahrenheit works beautifully), then your frozen water dilemma is solved.

If you will be keeping your rabbits outdoors, then it's important to provide fresh, unfrozen water to each rabbit at least twice each day. Offering additional hay is also important during cold weather; your rabbits will need to keep eating continually in order to stay warm. Provide protection for your outdoor hutches by keeping them out of direct wind.

In the summer, you are faced with an entirely different set of challenges. Rabbits are extremely sensitive to hot temperatures, and can deal with cold weather much more readily than they can hot weather. Always be sure to keep your hutches out of direct sunlight, and keep fans running if your rabbits are kept in a building. For added comfort during the hot summer days, you can take small plastic water bottles, fill them with water, and pop them in the freezer. Later, place one in each rabbit's cage, giving them an icy cold object to lie next to. This helps to keep your rabbits cool.

You can minimize your chances of being scratched by handling your rabbits properly. A rabbit that is afraid of being dropped will thrash about. In order to support your rabbit so that he feels safe, keep one hand around his shoulders and one hand underneath him. Always carry the rabbit close to your body so that he feels safe and protected.

While you *can* lift a rabbit from its cage by grasping the fur around the scruff of the neck and lifting, this really isn't the ideal manner. For one thing, you're neglecting to support his underside; for another thing, every time you lift a rabbit in this manner, you're loosening the flesh around the nape of the neck. This can be disastrous to a show animal.

**You have two primary objectives
when handling rabbits:
(1) keep your rabbit safe
and (2) don't get scratched.**

One helpful tip: when moving a rabbit in or out of his hutch, remember, bottom first. This means that if you're bringing the rabbit out of the hutch, spin him around so that you're bringing him out backward, with his hindquarters toward you.

Similarly, when it's time to put him back in his hutch, put him in hindquarters first. This is much easier than bringing him out or putting him back face first.

Take care to remove your rabbit bottom first from the hutch.

Buying Bunnies 101

You've prepared your facility and equipment, you've researched breeds and colors, you've considered all of your options, and now you're ready. It's time to buy bunnies!

In this chapter, we'll discuss how to find rabbits for sale, the financial aspects of purchasing rabbits, and the basics of selecting rabbits of top quality. We'll also outline questions you should ask and explain the importance of choosing pedigreed rabbits.

Where to Shop

When you're rabbit shopping, one of the most important things you can do is to buy from a reputable source. What, exactly, is a reputable source? Let's say that Tina is looking to buy a rabbit. She and her dad are out driving and see a sign that says "Rabbits 4 Sale." They decide to take a look.

The owner says that the rabbits are mixed breed and do not have pedigrees. Furthermore, the rabbits' hutches are in need of cleaning. The rabbits are cute, of course, but their noses have white goop on them. Their eyes are runny, and they don't seem very alert.

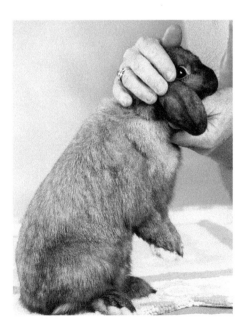

It's time to choose rabbits!

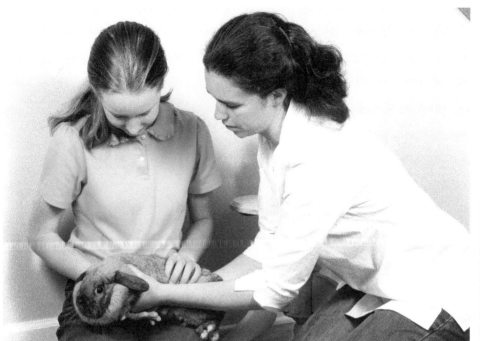

If you're buying your rabbits directly from a breeder, feel free to ask questions. Longtime breeders are knowledgeable and are usually gracious enough to share their wisdom.

Take time to get to know the rabbit you're thinking of purchasing. Look him over thoroughly and evaluate his personality. *Shutterstock*

Don't overlook the obvious—your own local 4-H or FFA club! Small animal sales, sponsored by 4-H or FFA, can be a wonderful place to locate rabbits.

Tina and her dad decide not to purchase any rabbits from this seller. Later, they answer a newspaper ad for "Pedigreed Mini Rex Rabbits for Sale" and visit the rabbitry. The hutches are clean and well maintained, the rabbits are healthy and cared for, and the rabbits are purebred, with pedigrees. Tina comes home with a top-quality Mini Rex, as well as some rabbit pellets (provided by the seller) and the rabbit's pedigree. Tina is happy, and so is her dad.

Like Tina, you'll want to buy from a seller who provides excellent care for the rabbits, has healthy stock, a clean facility, and a well-planned breeding program.

Classifieds

Check local newspapers for ads listing rabbits for sale. These ads are usually found in the "Pets" column, but you might also find rabbits listed under "Other Pets," if there are separate columns for dogs and cats.

Word of mouth

Ask your friends—especially other friends involved with 4-H or FFA rabbit projects. You may find that some of them have rabbits available for sale. Additionally, ask your leader for suggestions and recommendations on where to locate quality rabbits.

Internet

The World Wide Web can be a wonderful resource when you're searching for rabbits for sale. Take a look at the local ads on Craigslist; there are often rabbits listed for sale in the "Farm and Garden" category. Yahoo Groups are another helpful source, as many local rabbit clubs and breed associations have an active Yahoo Group where breeders can post listings

If you have your heart set on a particular breed, visit the website for the breed's specialty club and see if there are links to breeder websites in your area.

of rabbits for sale. And don't overlook the power of Google! If you type in "Mini Lop rabbit, for sale, Illinois," for example, you will undoubtedly find many websites of breeders with stock for sale.

Rabbit shows

Rabbit shows are an excellent place to purchase rabbits because you can view dozens—or hundreds! or thousands!—of rabbits for sale in one location at the same time. The rabbits offered at shows are typically sold by breeders of show rabbits, and so are usually rabbits of quality. They will almost always be purebred with pedigrees.

Livestock swaps

A livestock swap is a fun place to shop for animals, as well as a great place to meet and make friends and enjoy some fun. Livestock swaps are informal events where participants bring their livestock or related equipment to a meeting place to sell.

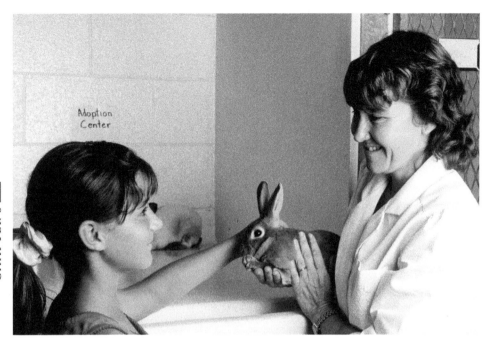

While it's very nice to consider adopting a rabbit from an animal shelter, be aware that the rabbit will probably be best suited to life as a pet. Most animal shelters cannot provide pedigrees for rabbits, which means that showing and breeding would not be good options.

If you want plenty of selection, visit an ARBA-sanctioned rabbit show and get ready to shop! There are dozens—if not hundreds—of rabbits for sale at an ARBA show, so take some time to look over the available selection.

These events are often held at a park or at a fairground, where interested individuals have the opportunity to browse and buy. A swap meet could be an excellent place for you to find rabbits locally.

Shipping Rabbits

It's possible that you won't be able to find what you're looking for locally. This is particularly true if you live in a remote or rural location, far from other rabbit

PUREBRED AND PEDIGREED

These are two words that will be very important to you when you are shopping for rabbits. In order to show at many open or county fair shows, your rabbits will need to be purebred with a pedigree. Don't confuse this with being *registered*, as this is an additional document and not vital for showing. Many shows require proof of pedigree. It's not enough for a seller to tell you that a rabbit is purebred; you need the proof of the pedigree on paper.

Additionally, you want to be careful not to lose your papers on a pedigreed rabbit. I can say this from experience, as I once misplaced the pedigree on one of my rabbits and couldn't locate it for several months. Don't let this happen to you! Keep your pedigrees filed away in a safe place.

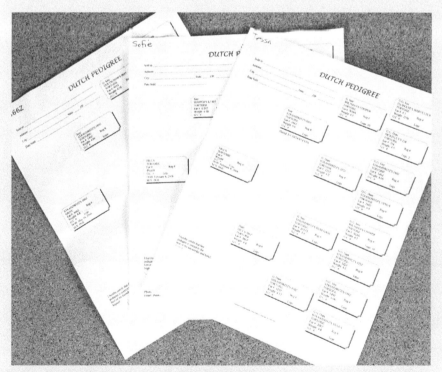

Here are some examples of computer-generated rabbit pedigrees. There are several computer programs available that are helpful for organizing your rabbitry records.

Animal swaps are another good possibility for finding rabbits locally. But keep in mind all of the regular criteria. You're looking for high-quality, healthy rabbits, purebred with pedigrees. Don't compromise!

There's nothing cuter than baby bunnies, but it can be difficult to ascertain their potential quality and type when they are very young. Ask for advice from a knowledgeable rabbit enthusiast in order to make the best choices.

breeders. This could also be true if you're interested in starting out with a rare or unusual breed. In this case, you might want to look into purchasing rabbits long-distance.

This isn't as difficult as it might sound; however, it is an expensive proposition. Shipping rabbits requires that they be sent via airplane from the seller to you, and there are several additional expenses that result. You will be responsible for paying for a rabbit carrier, the airline fees, and a health examination by a veterinarian. All in all, you should expect to pay several hundred dollars in additional expenses if you decide to ship rabbits via airline.

How Many to Start With?

A word of advice: don't start out with forty rabbits—or even ten. You want to enter your rabbit project slowly, so that you don't overwhelm yourself. I recommend starting with just a few rabbits, no more than four total. Pick a few different breeds. This variety will allow you to become acquainted with some of the different breed sizes, shapes, personalities, and other traits. After you've settled upon the breed that's right for you, you can sell the other rabbits and get down to the business of breeding.

The best way to begin a breeding program is by purchasing a trio for your initial investment. A trio of rabbits is a group of two does and one buck of the same breed. You'll be able to get used to owning rabbits on a small scale, while still having the necessary components to begin raising a few litters. The offspring are the basis of your rabbitry's future.

Once you have your breeding trio, you will not need to purchase any additional rabbits of that breed for the time being.

> The best way to begin a breeding program is by purchasing a trio for your initial investment. A trio of rabbits is a group of two does and one buck of the same breed.

For now, you'll want to concentrate simply on producing litters from your foundation does. From these litters, you will want to keep a few promising young rabbits for show or breeding purposes. If you can't determine the quality of your young rabbits in comparison to each other—or the breed's *Standard of Perfection*—then you'll want to enlist the help of a knowledgeable person to assist you in selecting the best youngsters from your litters.

What's next? You have your foundation trio and a good selection of youngsters, but they are all related. Your young rabbits are now nine months old, and you'd like to raise some litters from the young does—what do you do?

The time has come to purchase another buck. This purchase could be a bit trickier than your initial selection, as you need to choose a buck that is complementary to the faults and qualities of your foundation rabbits. This means that if your rabbits have consistent problems with a bad trait (poor markings in a Dutch, for example), you will want to diligently search for a new buck that is exemplary in this regard.

Selecting the Best

Choosing quality rabbits is important. You want your rabbits to be healthy, free of hereditary problems, and good examples of their breed. It goes without saying that if you plan to breed and show, you will want to select rabbits that are brood quality at the very least, and preferably show quality.

A trio (a buck and two does of the same breed) is an excellent way to get started with a small-scale bunny breeding program. Choose quality individuals with traits that are compatible.

But when you're new to rabbits, how can you tell a high-quality rabbit from a low-quality rabbit?

In this case, it's helpful to enlist the help of a more experienced rabbit enthusiast—perhaps your FFA project leader or a member of your 4-H club who has been involved with rabbits for a long time. Another great source of help can be found in the owner of the rabbits you're looking at buying: longtime breeders are usually knowledgeable about their stock and the breed in general, and they can give you excellent guidance, particularly regarding the specific animals you're considering. A knowledgeable breeder can provide you with a top-quality trio consisting of bloodlines that have a high probability of producing well together. This help can be extremely valuable.

You will also want to do your best to educate yourself. Purchase a copy of the *Standard of Perfection*. This wonderful book presents the breed standards for all forty-seven breeds recognized by the ARBA, and explains the ideal qualities and characteristics that are desired in each breed. Weights, colors, and markings are thoroughly explained. Additionally, you may want to study my previous book, *The Field Guide to Rabbits*, which includes full-color photographs of all forty-seven breeds, as well as an extensive guide to rabbit colors.

Rabbit shows are a wonderful learning experience, even if you're not showing.

UNDERSTANDING THE LINGO

Show type. Brood type. Pet type. You'll see many ads that mention these phrases, and you may find yourself scratching your head. What do they mean? What are the differences? At their most basic, the terms can be defined as follows:

- **Show Type**: The rabbit closely matches the breed's *Standard of Perfection* and is suitable for showing with no known disqualifications (DQs). It could also be used as a brood rabbit or a pet.

- **Brood Type**: The rabbit may not exactly match the breed's *Standard of Perfection*, but it matches closely enough to warrant being bred. It may have some type of DQ that would prevent showing, and it may be over or under the standard weight. It is also suitable as a pet. In the case of dwarf breeds, "false dwarfs" (dwarf rabbits without a dwarfing gene) are often sold as brood or pet type rather than show.

- **Pet Type**: While any rabbit has the potential to be a pet, when breeders sell "pet-type" animals, they are usually inferring that the rabbit doesn't have the quality to be a show specimen or a breeding animal. Pet-quality animals sometimes have DQs or do not match their breed's *Standard of Perfection*.

At first glance, these young Holland Lops appear to be quite similar, but slight differences in type are how the breeder will determine whether each one is show type, brood type, or pet quality.

QUESTIONS TO ASK WHEN BUYING RABBITS

Shutterstock

For all rabbits:

- How old is the rabbit?
- Purebred?
- Pedigreed?
- Ever been shown?
- Any health problems?
- Any DQs that would prevent showing?
- Any injuries?
- Weight?
- General disposition? (Outgoing and friendly? Reserved and shy?)
- What type of feed do you give? How much each day?
- Do you regularly feed hay? What type? How much?
- Do you use a water crock, an automatic waterer, or a water bottle?

For senior bucks:

- Has he ever sired any litters?

For senior does:

- Has she successfully raised any litters?
- How many kits did she produce?
- Was she a good mother?

Spend a few hours and quietly observe the judging. Take notes, listen to the judge's remarks, and try to evaluate the differences between the top rabbits and those placing further down the line. Before long, you'll be able to recognize the characteristics of a top-quality rabbit.

Health Considerations

This is very important, so listen closely: starting out with healthy rabbits is one of the most important things you can do when beginning your rabbit project. Don't settle for anything less than a healthy and hardy rabbit. You'll want your rabbits to have bright eyes and noses that are free of anything drippy. You don't want to purchase a rabbit that sneezes, as this can

Learn all you can before you buy your first rabbits. If you take the time to educate yourself, you'll be able to make well-informed decisions about stock selection.

be a sign of allergies or "snuffles." Rabbits should be in good condition (not too thin and not obese, either). Look for rabbits that have healthy coats and are clean (flip each bunny over; you don't want to see dried manure stuck in his fur).

Age Considerations

Should you start out with young rabbits or older ones? The answer depends on your intentions. If you're looking for show specimens, then starting out with junior rabbits rather than senior rabbits is a perfectly good option. If you don't plan to show your rabbits but do want to breed them, keep in mind that rabbits generally need to be at least six months old before you can consider breeding them. Starting

out with eight-week-old bunnies means that you'll have a few months of waiting before you can begin raising litters of your own—but sometimes it's good to own your rabbits for a few months before you begin adding more. This lets you get used to the daily care and responsibility that comes with rabbit ownership.

How old is *too* old? Rabbits do not generally have long life expectancies. Domestic rabbits typically live for eight to ten years, but a rabbit's age can have a significant impact on its success at shows. Rabbits over the age of two or three years old are often considered too old to be competitive at shows. Additionally, fertility rates decrease in older rabbits, so keep this in mind when choosing stock. This is

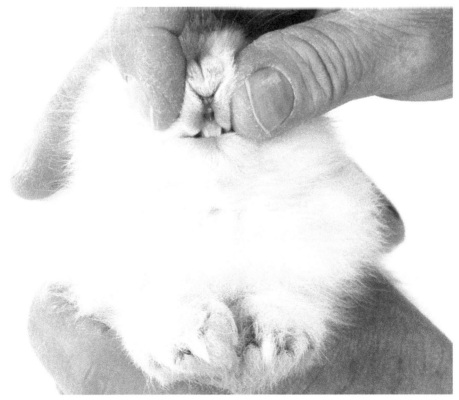

Choosing healthy rabbits is of paramount importance. Check for proper teeth alignment and make sure that the rabbit isn't exhibiting signs of illness.

not to say that older rabbits won't win on the show table or that they can't produce litters, only that the odds decrease.

How Much to Spend?

The price of rabbits varies widely, so it's impossible to give you a specific guideline or range. Prices vary from breed to breed, and also within breeds. Prices are affected by a number of factors: quality, color, type, markings, and size. The highest price tag I've seen on a rabbit is $350; I've also seen rabbits for free. You'll find plenty of very nice bunnies to pick from in the $15 to $50 range; this is especially true if you're buying junior rabbits. Proven senior show rabbits will typically command higher prices.

I was recently shopping for a new Holland Lop buck. I wanted something of excellent quality, but I specifically wanted a buck with a top-notch crown and massive bone (meaning bone that is heavy for the size of the rabbit). I also wanted a buck with the "broken" color pattern. I looked for quite a while, browsing breeders' websites, asking around, looking at shows. I ended up finding an eight-week-old fellow for sale at a show. He met my criteria, and as a bonus, he also had the bloodlines that I was hoping to find to complement my program. This buck was priced at $50. Others I had looked at ranged in price from $25 to $175. The moral of this story? The $175 rabbit didn't have the specific qualities I was looking for, even though he was truly lovely in his own way. I just found the qualities that I was seeking in a $50 bunny. A higher price doesn't always mean that it's the very best for what *you* need. Always make sure that you focus on finding a rabbit with the qualities that you need for your specific program, rather than assuming that an expensive rabbit is always better.

Young rabbits, known as juniors when they are less than six months old (*above*), can be a wise choice when you're just starting out; they are usually less expensive than senior rabbits. But don't purchase any rabbit that is less than eight weeks old. This two-week-old Rex kit (*right*) is too young to leave its mother.

YOUTH, 4-H, OR FFA DISCOUNTS

Many rabbit breeders recognize the fact that 4-H and FFA participants are often doing their projects on a limited budget. You may not have hundreds of dollars at your disposal to invest in your rabbit project. For this reason, breeders sometimes offer a youth, 4-H, or FFA discount, particularly if you purchase multiple rabbits from them. These discounts vary, but they can add up to significant savings and might make a big difference in the quality of rabbits that you're able to afford. While not all rabbit breeders offer this type of discount, it doesn't hurt to politely ask them if they offer a youth, 4-H, or FFA discount. If the answer is "no," you can decide whether the rabbits are within your budget or not. However, chances are you'll be able to find many breeders who are eager to encourage young rabbit enthusiasts and seek to help in any way they can.

Rabbit prices can vary widely, but always try to purchase the highest quality that you can afford.

SHOW ME THE (BUNNY) MONEY

It seems logical that a smaller rabbit will be less expensive to maintain than a larger rabbit, but exactly how does this translate to dollars and cents? Here's a project that can help you to determine the exact cost of keeping rabbits of varying sizes.

Start out with three rabbits of different sizes: a small or dwarf rabbit, such as a Holland Lop; a medium-sized rabbit, such as a Lilac; and a large or giant rabbit, such as a Californian. For one month, keep detailed records of the maintenance costs of each rabbit. Be sure to include startup costs for cages or hutches (these vary in price depending on size) as well as daily care expenses for feed and hay.

At the end of the month, calculate the cost of keeping each rabbit and evaluate the results. Was the larger rabbit considerably more expensive to maintain than the smaller rabbits? Was there a significant difference between the cost of keeping a small rabbit versus a medium-sized rabbit? Or were the cost differences negligible? This information will be beneficial to you as you make decisions about your rabbit project in the future. Compare the expenses with the potential of income: will you be able to sell the offspring of the larger rabbits for a higher price than the offspring of the medium-sized rabbits? Does a certain breed sell for a particularly good price in your area?

Shutterstock

Daily Rabbit Care

R abbits require daily care. They need fresh food and water each day, as well as daily observation to watch for any unexpected health issues that might arise. In this chapter, we'll discuss the ins and outs of feeding bunnies, from hay and pellets to water and treats. We'll also discuss other parts of your daily rabbit schedule, like tidying up and evaluating your rabbits. Let's begin!

The Bunny Diet

Hay

Quality hay is the backbone of your rabbit feeding program, despite what you might hear or read otherwise. While pellets are a vital aspect of a rabbit's diet, too, they must be supplemented with hay. Ideally, you should offer hay "free choice," which means that you provide your rabbits with as much hay as they will eat. Experiment with how much until you find an amount that allows your rabbits to have 24/7 access to hay while not providing so much that there is excess waste.

In order to keep your rabbits' digestive systems healthy, you'll want to feed them a consistent diet each day. Avoid sudden changes to feed amounts or types.

Hay, a basic bunny food, is essential for promoting top digestive health. You can select alfalfa hay or grass hay, but if you're feeding unlimited amounts of hay to your rabbits, grass hay is probably the better choice.

Finding quality hay is of prime importance. Small square bales are a cost-effective way to purchase hay, although you will need sufficient space to store the hay.

Hay is messy to feed, but the benefits far outweigh the inconvenience. It provides your rabbits with an excellent source of fiber, which is an enormous help toward preventing gastrointestinal problems such as GI stasis. Fiber also helps to keep the gut flora healthy.

Another benefit of hay is that it provides your rabbits with an opportunity to chew. This helps to alleviate boredom, as well as giving rabbits the chance to wear down their ever-growing teeth.

But what kind of hay should you feed? Generally speaking, there are two types of hay: grass hay and alfalfa. Many breeders recommend grass hay for optimal health, while others vow that alfalfa hay is preferable. Grass hay proponents often cite potential digestive problems or diarrhea that can occur after feeding alfalfa hay to rabbits. On the other hand, alfalfa proponents report better body condition with their alfalfa-fed rabbits, while experiencing no problems with alfalfa feeding. Your choice may be determined by whichever type of hay is most readily available in your area. Given the choice, most rabbits will prefer alfalfa hay over grass hay—but this is not always the case. Personally, I feed grass hay to my rabbits, but I recently offered a small tidbit of alfalfa hay to one of my does as a treat. She wouldn't touch it. She looked, she sniffed, and she rejected. She simply wanted her regular grass hay.

If you are feeding your hay free-choice, then you can feel more comfortable in allowing your rabbits unlimited access to hay if you're feeding grass hay. Because there is no risk of digestive problems from the consumption of grass hay, bunnies can enjoy an "all-you-can-eat" situation; this wouldn't be advisable with alfalfa hay.

Beyond variety, it's even more important to be sure that you're purchasing *quality* hay. The importance of this cannot be overstated: you must have hay that is clean, sweet-smelling, and free of mold or excess dust. Always discard any hay that is contaminated with mold, as well as any hay that contained any deceased creatures (such as mice or snakes). If you come across any of these contaminants in your hay, do not feed it to your rabbits.

You can purchase small square bales of hay; undoubtedly this is the most cost-effective way to feed hay to your rabbits.

Rabbits can be fussy about their water, sometimes refusing to drink if the water tastes slightly different than what they are used to. For this reason, you may have difficulty in getting your rabbits to drink when you take them to a show. Most rabbits will tolerate the taste of bottled spring water, so you can purchase a case of bottled water to take along to shows.

However, if you have only a few rabbits, or don't have access to the small square bales in your area, rabbit supply companies and feed stores carry pre-packaged hay in small quantities. This is usually a more expensive way to purchase hay, but you may find it more convenient.

Water

Next, we come to water—also vitally important. Your rabbits must have continuous access to fresh, clean water. As previously discussed, you can provide water for your rabbits in crocks, cups, bottles, or through an automatic watering system. Whatever your preferred method of presentation, the important thing is to provide fresh water daily. This is vital for any rabbit but doubly so for lactating does (female rabbits nursing litters). A nursing doe has a considerably higher need for water in order to compensate for the loss of hydration due to nursing the litter.

One tip: if you use water bottles, you know that they are mounted on the outside of the cage with the nozzle extending into the interior of the cage. You will always want to make sure that the nozzle hasn't been accidentally pushed out of the cage by your rabbit.

If you decide to provide water in bottles, always be sure that your rabbits are utilizing the bottles before removing their water crocks. While most rabbits enjoy drinking from water bottles, there are some individuals who just won't use them, so don't assume anything until you have actually observed the rabbit drinking from the bottle.

Pellets make up an important portion of your rabbits' daily fare. While the variety of commercially produced pellets can seem a bit bewildering, if you do your homework, you'll be able to select a brand and formula that will be suitable for your feeding program.

I say this because I have seen it happen—at first glance, it looks as though the bunny's water doesn't need refilling, when actually they can't drink because the nozzle isn't accessible. Always check all of your water bottles and crocks at least two times a day.

Pellets

Pellets are also a vital component of your rabbits' diet. Rabbit pellets are commercially produced by many companies, and if you query other rabbit breeders, you will undoubtedly hear positive and negative experiences on all of the different brands and varieties.

There are many kinds of feed: show formulas, pro formulas, and so on. What's the difference? How do you choose?

Oftentimes it comes down to ingredients. Some formulas contain corn; others are corn-free. The level of protein can vary widely between types, typically from 12 to 18 percent protein. You are probably safe in selecting a mid-range protein, such as 14 or 16 percent (I feed a 16 percent pellet). Many people feel that higher protein levels (in the 18 percent range) are too high and can cause diarrhea. Others feel that an 18 percent feed can be a beneficial boost to rapidly growing junior rabbits.

Also check the fiber content on the feed label. Fiber is an essential part of your rabbits' diet, so the higher the percentage of fiber, the better. Aim for at least 18 percent, and higher figures are even more important if for some reason you are not feeding hay.

Homemade Grain Mixes

Maybe you don't want to purchase commercial pellets for your rabbits, and you'd prefer to formulate your own rabbit

> **The rule of thumb for basic rabbit feeding is one ounce of pellets per pound of body weight per day.**

feed. Popular homemade choices include mixes of oatmeal, sunflower seeds, barley, and grains.

One thing to remember is that commercial rabbit feeds contain precise amounts of fiber and protein, so you know that your rabbits are receiving ample quantities of these important nutrients. Additionally, some rabbit feeds contain other additions, such as papaya, which helps to prevent fur blockage in the intestine (particularly beneficial for the longhaired Angora breeds). Now, you can certainly feed papaya tablets as an addition to your homemade grain mixture, but it is important to make sure that you think through everything you might want to add to your homemade mixture.

If you want to feed your rabbits some particular ingredient, such as sunflower seeds, you can add it to the commercial pellet mix, or you can feed commercial pellets in the morning and then feed sunflower seeds in the evening. There are a multitude of possibilities to consider.

How Much to Feed?

Your next question is inevitable: *How much should I feed each individual rabbit?*

There isn't an easy answer to this question, as there are so many variables, but you will soon get the hang of determining feed amounts for your bunnies.

The rule of thumb for basic rabbit feeding is one ounce of pellets per pound of body weight per day. In other words, if you're feeding a nine-pound Rex rabbit,

How much should you feed your rabbit? Not this much! This rabbit's bowl is filled with too much food for this small rabbit to consume. If left unattended, the remaining food would go to waste before he was able to finish it.

you might use nine ounces of feed per day as your base figure. (If you feed two times a day, as I do, then you'll split this amount and feed half at each feeding.) After some time on the nine-ounce ration, ask yourself: Is my rabbit the correct weight? Or is she gaining too much weight? Becoming too thin? You will then adjust your rabbit's ration accordingly.

There are exceptions, of course. Mature bucks and non-lactating does may need a smaller amount of pellets in order to stay in prime condition and not become overweight. A lactating doe will need increased feed in order to support her growing litter. Newly weaned baby rabbits should have lower amounts of pelleted feed and higher amounts of hay, while rabbits in the three- to six-month range are like little bottomless pits. They should have access to increased rations in order to keep up with their rate of growth. In general, rabbits that are too thin should receive increased feed; rabbits that are too fat should receive fewer pellets. While you never want your rabbits to be thin, you really don't want them to be overweight either. Overweight does can have reduced fertility rates, so try to ensure that your breeding does are in prime condition.

Watch to make sure that your rabbits are eating all of the pellets you provide. If you come back for your evening feeding and there are still uneaten pellets in the feeders, you may be feeding too much. Dispose of the uneaten feed. Don't just leave leftovers for your bunnies to eat "later"—they won't. Feed that has been sitting out for several hours (or overnight) becomes very unappetizing to a bunny. Also remember to store your rabbit feed in containers with lids; this keeps the feed clean, dry, and fresh. Clean metal trash cans are rodent-proof and work perfectly for storing feed.

Fruits and Vegetables

"An apple a day" is good advice for humans and can be good advice for bunnies as well—in moderation, of course. Certain fruits and vegetables are good choices for rabbit treats, including apples, carrots, pears, raspberries, strawberries, and lettuce (not iceberg lettuce, however).

Most rabbits find carrots to be an enjoyable treat. *Shutterstock*

HELP! MY BUNNY WON'T EAT!

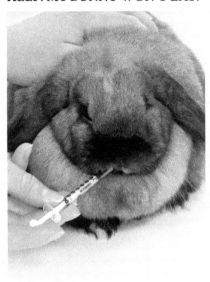

If your rabbit continues to refuse food or water, you may need to begin administering liquids via a syringe.

This is not as unusual as you might think, and can be caused by a variety of factors. The very first thing to do is to make sure that your rabbit has water. If rabbits do not have water, they will not eat. Has she tipped over her water crock? Is her water bottle working properly? Check the nozzle to make sure that it isn't somehow clogged. Is the water fresh and clean?

If the water situation is not the problem, then take a look at the feed itself. Has the feed gotten wet? Does it have an odd smell? Is the hay fresh and sweet-smelling, or is it dusty and foul-smelling? If all appears well with the feed, then it's time to move on to the bunny herself.

How does she look? Is she bright and happy? Or is she lying around her cage, breathing heavily? Check for any bloating (you can't miss it—their little bodies become firm and heavy, expanding around the abdomen).

If she's bright-looking and alert, then she may just not be hungry at the moment. Refresh her food and water, and perhaps offer her a small bit of a treat (a small piece of apple or a few blades of grass) to entice her appetite. Sometimes a rabbit just isn't hungry and will begin eating again in a short time.

Another thing to check: her teeth. If a rabbit has developed malocclusion of the teeth (not uncommon, especially in growing juniors), her teeth may have become so overgrown that eating has become difficult. In this case, her teeth will need to be trimmed.

If your rabbit looks sick, it is quite a bit more concerning. Having said that, I have had bunnies that have looked lethargic and unhappy at seven o'clock in the morning, and then suddenly jumped up and begun eating two hours later, without any further complications or exhibitions of illness. But I've also had experiences where they didn't bounce back as quickly. In these situations, you may be dealing with GI stasis, which is a dangerous slowing down or stoppage of the gastrointestinal system. Contact a veterinarian, because GI stasis can be fatal.

In the meantime, your primary objective is to entice the rabbit to begin eating. You can do this by offering her favorite treats, but this isn't always effective. Hydration is important, because you want to jumpstart the rabbit's stalled digestion by keeping things moving in its intestine. A small syringe (without a needle, of course) can be filled with water and then slowly deposited into the rabbit's mouth. This isn't difficult, but you want to be very careful not to choke the rabbit. Go slowly, administering a few drops at a time.

Dandelions are wildly popular with my rabbits, but they also enjoy plain ol' grass. With all of these "green" or "fruity" treats, the key to remember is to proceed slowly. Always introduce new treats in small amounts over the course of several days, increasing slowly until you are feeding the amount you desire. Abruptly changing your rabbit's diet can cause digestive problems, so please be careful.

These baby rabbits are too young to eat dandelions, vegetables, or other greens, as these items increase the risk of developing enteritis. Wait until they are six months old to introduce greens to their diet. *Shutterstock*

Another thing to remember: many people believe that the feeding of greens, including fruits and vegetables, can be detrimental to junior rabbits (under six months of age). Because junior rabbits are already at increased risk of enteritis (see pages 94–95), it's probably wiser to withhold fruits, vegetables, and dandelions until they have reached at least six months of age. (Remember, if you're feeding any of these to your does, remove them before their nursing litters pop out of the nest boxes and try to taste them.)

One more point to remember: If you're gathering grass or dandelions for your rabbits from your yard, make sure that they weren't picked from an area that has been sprayed with any type of chemical. This could be poisonous to your rabbits.

Rabbit treats should be fed only in very small amounts. A small yogurt treat or a small portion of a bread slice can make a fun rabbit treat.

If you decide to pick greens or dandelions for your rabbits, always be sure that you have selected them from an area that has not been sprayed with any pesticides or other harmful chemicals.

Other Treats

Bread is a popular treat with some rabbits, although I have not had much success in offering it to my own bunnies. You'll probably find that your rabbits will jump for joy over anything sweet, such as a yogurt drop (a type of commercial rabbit treat). However, you'll want to limit the number of sugary treats that you offer your rabbits; a small piece of apple is usually a better choice.

Exercise

All bunnies benefit from regular exercise. If you keep your rabbitry numbers at an easily manageable level, you'll be able to provide this opportunity for your rabbits on a regular basis.

You can purchase a harness and leash for your rabbit and literally take him for a walk, just as you would a dog. The downside to this method of exercise is that most rabbits don't particularly enjoy being taken for walks. They are usually more interested in leaps and darts than they are in calmly walking at a steady pace, but you can certainly give it a try; perhaps your rabbit will enjoy the process. One note of caution: make sure that the harness is properly fitted—not too loose and not too tight. It's possible for a rabbit to squeeze out of a harness if the fittings aren't snug enough, and then you have a bunny on the loose. Catching a loose rabbit is not an easy task.

An exercise pen is a great way to allow your rabbit some play time while keeping him safe at the same time. You can fashion an exercise pen from a wooden frame with hardware cloth, or you can

A harness and leash can be a safe and easy way to exercise your rabbit. Just be sure that you keep your walks short enough that your rabbits don't become overheated. *Shutterstock*

Your rabbits will enjoy the opportunity to cavort in an exercise pen. This Holland Lop is kicking up her heels in delight.

purchase prefabricated exercise pens made especially for rabbits. I use a portable dog pen, which works quite well, but I always stay and keep an eye on my rabbits while they play.

With an exercise pen, your main concern is to keep your rabbit from escaping, so obviously a pen with an enclosed floor is the safest bet. Otherwise, make sure that the sides meet the ground and that there are no gaps through which a cunning bunny could squeeze. Also be sure to watch for predators. Keep an eye on your rabbits at all times while they are outdoors. Watch for snakes, dogs, raccoons, and birds (these might attack from above).

Also be aware of exposing your rabbits to the elements: Direct sun can be very harmful and can cause heat stroke and other disastrous problems. Wind and rain also have negative effects on rabbits, so be aware of those as well.

Once you have taken care of all of the danger areas, sit back and enjoy the show as your rabbits cavort, play, kick up their heels, and have fun. It's a treat for you—and them!

FEED COMPARISONS

If you'd like to try an interesting experiment, work on a feed comparison to determine which one produces the best results in your rabbits. Early in the spring, take two rabbits that you may wish to enter in a show later in the season. It helps if the rabbits are from the same litter, since this eliminates the variables of age and breed, but you can use unrelated rabbits if you wish. Then select two different types of rabbit food. You might decide to feed one rabbit a pellet with 16 percent protein and feed the other rabbit a pellet with 18 percent protein. Or perhaps you might choose to feed one rabbit a commercial formula and the other rabbit a homemade grain mixture.

After a few weeks, compare the rabbits. Is one rabbit in significantly better condition than the other? Does one have firmer flesh or better fur quality? If you can determine that one type of feed produced a more positive result, then you might decide to switch all or most of your rabbits to that type of feed.

A clean hutch is a healthy environment for your rabbits. Regularly remove all soiled hay and droppings, so that your hutches remain clean and dry.

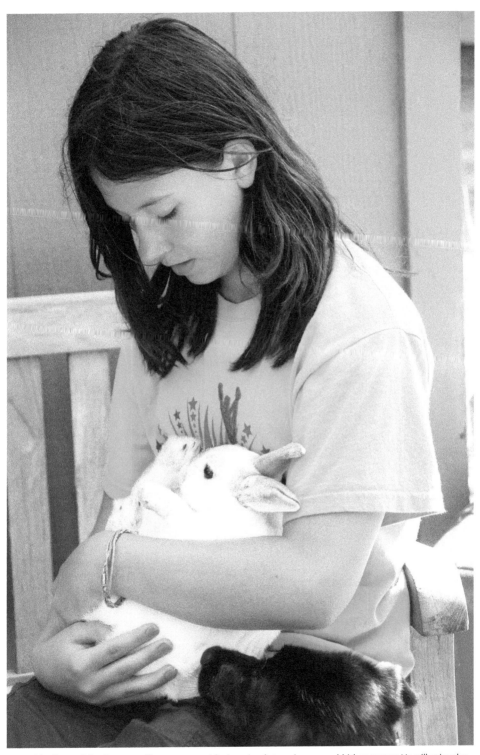

Even with all your daily chores, you'll want to set aside time simply to enjoy your rabbit's company. He will enjoy the attention, too!

Cleanliness

While feeding and providing fresh water for your rabbits are the backbone of your daily chores, it's also important to dedicate a portion of time each day toward keeping your rabbitry tidy. Empty the trays underneath the cages, and remove the droppings, urine, and any spilled pellets or hay. (I give the trays a quick rinse with water to wash away the residue.) Next, check the condition of the cage interiors. Clean out any soiled hay and any droppings that might not have fallen through the wire floor. If your rabbits have nest boxes, check to see that they are clean inside.

The water bottles or crocks will also need attention. Regular cleaning is important to maintaining health in your rabbitry. The feeders will also need occasional cleaning; be sure to dispose of any "fines" (dusty, crumbled pellets) that remain in the bottom of your feeders.

Don't overlook the floor! Hay can be quite messy, so sweep around your cages regularly. (Don't forget to clean behind the cages too; hay always seems to multiply back there!) At the same time, you can sweep up any spilled droppings or bits of feed. Keeping your floors free of spilled feed helps to minimize rodent problems in your barn and also helps to

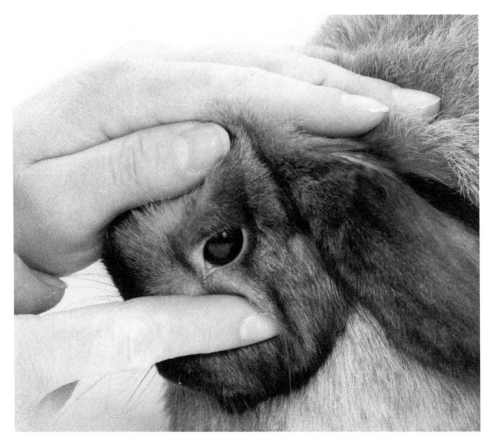

Watch for runny eyes, "snotty" noses, sneezing, or lack of appetite; these can be indicative of illness.

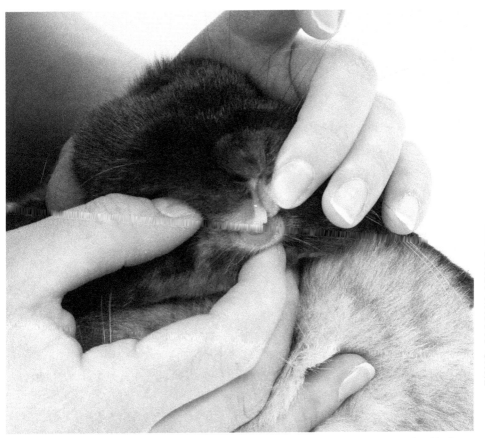

While this is not something that you will do every day, it is wise to check your rabbits' teeth regularly. If a rabbit has misaligned teeth, it may have difficulty eating and the teeth may need to be trimmed.

keep other critters away if you're keeping your rabbits outdoors.

Occasionally, you will want to do a thorough cleaning of your cages and equipment. You can use a diluted bleach solution (one part bleach to sixteen parts water) to disinfect the cages, then rinse thoroughly and leave them in the direct sun to dry. If you'd rather not use bleach, you can purchase Vanodine, which is a product highly recommended for disinfecting rabbit equipment, feeders, and waterers. You can purchase Vanodine from rabbit supply companies.

Some choose to disinfect quite frequently (every few weeks), while others aim for once or twice annually. It really depends on the individual situation and whether or not there is incidence of disease in the rabbitry.

Daily Bunny Check

You'll want to do a daily bunny check. This means taking a close look at each and every bunny in your rabbitry. Make sure that everyone looks bright and happy, that they are all eating happily, and that nothing abnormal is going on. Be on the lookout for unexplained diarrhea, lethargic rabbits, injuries, or disinterest in food. Of course, there are exceptions to the rule. I have occasionally had rabbits that simply will not eat while they are being watched. While every other bunny in the barn is jumping for joy over their dinner, these sulky bunnies will huddle in the back corner of their hutch, seemingly ignoring everything that goes on. I'll fill their feeder with fresh feed. No reaction. I'll give them a pile of delightful hay. No response. Yet when I return to the barn later in the day, their feeder is empty and the hay has disappeared. So, obviously they eat; I just never see them do it. Thus, you should try not to worry if you have the occasional rabbits that aren't overly excited to see their food. As long as they're eating and finishing up their meals, don't worry.

You will also use the daily check to evaluate the current condition of your bunnies. Pick them up, flip them over, and check their bottoms. Some rabbits (junior Holland Lops are notorious for this) can get quite messy when their night feces get stuck in their fur. As unpleasant as it sounds, it is something you'll need to check for regularly and deal with as necessary. The dirty areas can be removed with scissors (find a helper and be careful not to inadvertently clip your bunny instead of his fur!), or you can try to soak the "chunks" off with warm water. Keeping the cages very clean can help to minimize this problem, but it is not always enough to prevent it entirely.

Don't overlook your rabbits' toenails. Check them regularly, and trim as necessary. You can purchase nail trimmers from rabbit supply companies, although you can get by with a tiny pair of nail trimmers for dogs, if necessary. Never let your rabbits' toenails become too long.

CHAPTER 4

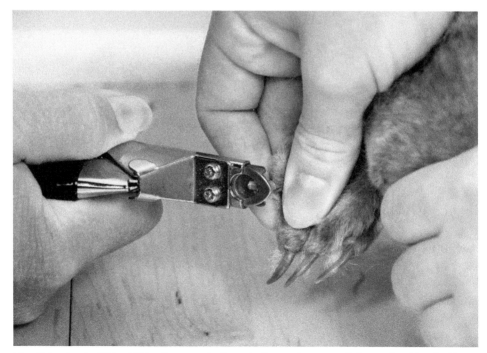

It's nail trimming time! This rabbit's nails are overdue for a trim; be sure that you regularly attend to this task with your rabbits.

86

Rabbits have thick coats and can sometimes appear to be in better condition than they really are. A quick feel of your rabbit's body can give you a much clearer idea of its true condition.

Lethargy can be a sign of illness, but sometimes rabbits are simply enjoying a bit of a rest. Is his appetite good? Is he drinking well? These are other things to keep in mind.

Healthy Bunnies

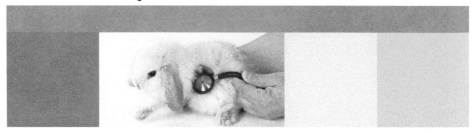

A healthy rabbit is a happy rabbit—in other words, a rabbit that is eager for its meals, bright-eyed, active, and alert. A healthy rabbit exhibits lustrous fur and produces normal droppings. Diarrhea, lack of appetite, fur that is dull or rough, or a lethargic appearance can be signs of illness. Also watch for increased respiration, teeth grinding, or any appearance of bloating, as all of these can also be signs of an ill rabbit.

Keeping your rabbits healthy is undoubtedly your primary concern.

Thankfully, most of the time, rabbits are remarkably healthy creatures. This chapter addresses some of the most commonly seen medical issues that can arise, so you'll be prepared in the event that one occurs in your rabbitry. We'll also discuss how to find a knowledgeable veterinarian to care for your bunnies. For more detailed medical information, I recommend purchasing a rabbit medical guide, or refer to the ARBA's fine *Official Guide Book: Raising Better Rabbits and Cavies* (guinea pigs), which is available for free when you join the ARBA.

Help! My Rabbit Is Sneezing!

I'm listing this first, because it's one of the most common problems seen by rabbit owners. In rabbit circles, it's common knowledge that a sneezing rabbit is an upsetting and potentially threatening situation for your rabbitry. So what should you do if one of your rabbits begins sneezing?

The first step is to isolate the sneezing bunny, at least temporarily. Observe the rabbit for a few days. Does the sneezing continue? Or was it a single event? Is there white discharge dripping from his nostrils? Are his eyes watering? If his nostrils are clean and the sneezing does not continue,

The picture of health! This rabbit is bright, alert, and in excellent body condition, and he has the appetite to prove it.

dusty hay, perhaps, or a dusty environment. Some rabbits are chronic sneezers while never exhibiting further symptoms or infecting any other rabbits. Some breeders feel these are simply allergic rabbits; others believe they are carriers of pasteurella, more commonly known as snuffles. If the sneezing persists and is accompanied by thick discharge, the diagnosis is likely snuffles.

Snuffles is, unfortunately, a common illness in rabbits and extremely contagious. Some rabbits carry it without showing symptoms, although symptoms can suddenly appear, often after a rabbit has been stressed in some way (such as being moved to a new location, taken to a show, or delivering a litter). Treatment is possible with antibiotics, but the success rate is variable. It is generally felt that the illness can sometimes be put in remission, but most experts believe that it cannot be cured. Some breeders cull diligently for snuffles; you may or may not wish to do this. If you choose not to cull, then isolation is key: Keep a snuffly bunny separated from the rest of your herd! And don't feed or handle your other rabbits after handling a rabbit with snuffles; always care for that one last, and then wash your hands to prevent spreading germs.

it may have been a simple, innocent event, and it may be nothing more than that. In this case, you can probably be safe in returning your rabbit to the herd after a few sneeze-free days.

On the other hand, let's say that the sneezing continues but isn't accompanied by any nasal discharge. This could possibly be an allergic reaction to something:

If you choose not to cull, then isolation is key: Keep a snuffly bunny separated from the rest of your herd!

Clean, dry nostrils—just what the doctor ordered. Watch for discharge coming from your rabbit's nostrils; this is a sign of pastuerella (snuffles).

Parasites

Oh boy, now we get to discuss this unpleasant topic. Get ready, everybody. There are two types of parasites that can affect your rabbits: internal parasites and external parasites. Let's learn more about each type.

Internal parasites

Coccidia is a type of internal parasite that you will hear mentioned regularly by rabbit breeders. It infects the liver and intestines and is frequently seen in rabbits. Other intestinal parasites that can be problematic for rabbits include pinworms, tapeworms, and whipworms. Talk to your veterinarian about whether you should deworm your rabbits. Many breeders recommend a once or twice yearly Ivermectin dewormer treatment; however, the FDA has not approved this usage, and the dosage must be carefully determined as to prevent accidental overdose.

It is not usually possible to detect intestinal parasites visually; therefore

Ear mites can be treated with mineral oil, or you can purchase special ear medication that is formulated to fight ear mites.

you will want to do your best to prevent infestations of these organisms (such as coccidia) in the first place by maintaining a scrupulously clean environment for your rabbits. Coccidia can be diagnosed post-mortem; it is obvious due to the presence of visible white spots on the liver. Never eat meat from rabbits that were infected with coccidiosis.

If you decide that a coccidiosis treatment is necessary for your rabbits, you might consider using sulfaquinoxaline, a treatment that is often prescribed by veterinarians for cattle and sheep that have coccidiosis. Again, talk to your veterinarian before administering any medication to your rabbits.

External parasites

External parasites that can affect rabbits include fleas, ear mites, and fur mites. Just as with your dog or cat, your rabbits can become infested with fleas. If you determine that fleas are an issue in your rabbitry, then ask your veterinarian about using flea and tick products on your rabbits (make sure to inquire about proper dosages). Fur mites can cause itching and hair loss in rabbits, especially around the rabbit's head and neck, so watch for these indications. Flea powder for cats can be effective in treating ear mites, but again, ask your vet for advice and dosages.

Perhaps you've noticed that one of your rabbits has a crusty, scabby substance on the inside of its ear. This is ear canker, which is an outer ear infection caused by ear mites. (This can be slightly confusing, since ear canker is actually on the inside of their ear, but it is called this to differentiate it from an actual inner-ear

Mites and fleas are types of external parasites that can affect your rabbits; watch out for abnormal amounts of scratching. *Shutterstock*

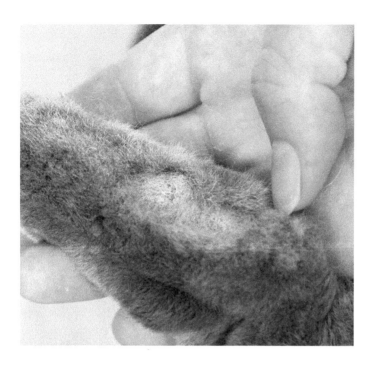

Regularly check your rabbits' feet for sore hocks. If you notice that one of your rabbits has developed this condition, the spots should be treated with an antibiotic ointment, and you should also provide the rabbit with a comfortable place to sit, such as a floor mat.

infection, which would not be on the exposed part of the ear, but rather inside the head.) You can treat ear canker with vegetable or mineral oil, carefully depositing a drop or two in each ear for a few days. Some breeders also utilize this treatment as a preventative, treating all of their rabbits' ears with oil every few weeks.

Sore Hocks

This problem (characterized by crusty, weepy sores) is found on the bottom of a rabbit's hind feet. It can be caused by sitting for prolonged periods of time on the wire floor of a hutch. It can occur in any breed of rabbit, but Rex rabbits seem to be slightly more susceptible to sore hocks than some of the other breeds. Sore hocks should be treated with an antibiotic ointment (Preparation H is commonly used), but it may take time for the wounds to heal and new fur to grow

in again. Prevention is also important. Supply resting boards in your hutches to provide a comfortable place for each rabbit to sit and to improve or prevent cases of sore hocks.

Mastitis

As we will discuss further in Chapter 7, mastitis is an infection of the mammary glands that can occur in breeding does. It is characterized by swelling, heat, and redness in the teat areas. Treatment requires penicillin injections, although hot packs can also prove effective.

Slowly weaning a litter can help to prevent the occurrence of mastitis. This method allows the doe's milk supply to slowly diminish as the litter is gradually weaned. If you were to suddenly wean an entire litter of eight kits, then the doe would be left producing an ample milk supply with no kits to relieve the pressure; this is when mastitis usually

Always check your does regularly for mastitis after kindling, during their lactation period, and after weaning. Be vigilant so that you can immediately treat as necessary.

occurs. It's important to remember, however, that a doe can sometimes develop mastitis immediately after giving birth too. In any case, check your does regularly after kindling (giving birth), during the weeks of nursing, and particularly right after weaning. Be aware of any changes, swelling, heat, or pain in her teats.

Enteritis and GI Stasis

Rabbits are susceptible to two serious intestinal problems: mucoid enteritis and gastrointestinal (GI) stasis.

Enteritis is an inflammation of the intestines. It is commonly seen in baby rabbits, especially those that have been recently weaned. Affected rabbits develop diarrhea and can become listless, and the

condition is often fatal if not attended to promptly. You can reduce your rabbits' chances of developing enteritis by making all dietary changes very slowly (especially for rabbits under twelve weeks of age), delaying the introduction of green foods until after six months of age, and providing ample quantities of hay.

GI stasis is a slowing down or stoppage of the intestines. It is a

It's best to wait until baby rabbits are six months old before introducing fresh greens into their diet. For this reason, you might want to limit their time in an exercise pen if they are trying to nibble on grass. *Shutterstock*

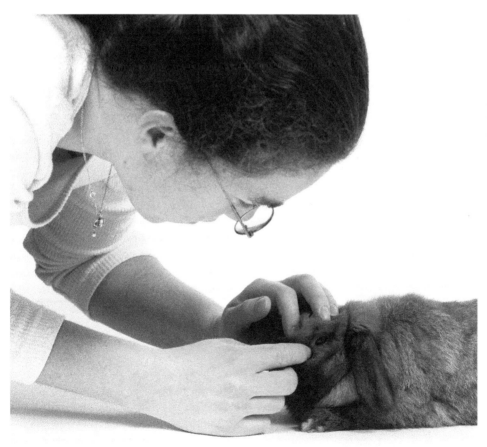

A lack of appetite or lethargy can be indicative of gastrointestinal stasis (known as GI stasis). You will need to seek veterinary assistance promptly.

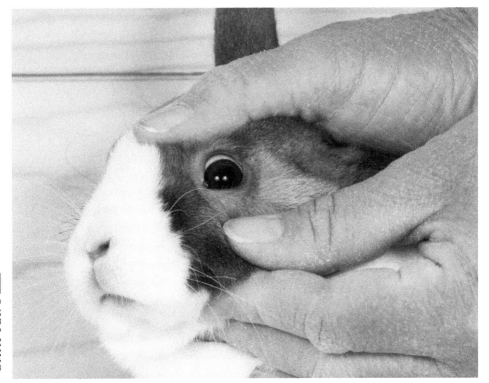

Baby rabbits are at an increased risk of developing "sore eyes." Be sure to check the eyes of your young kits regularly. This kit has healthy eyes.

dangerous illness, although many have had success with treating it. Signs include listlessness, lack of appetite, a dull coat, failure to drink, and bloating. Often the rabbit ceases to produce droppings. Treatment must begin promptly (see "Help! My Bunny Won't Eat!" on page 78 for treatment information).

It's wise to keep simethicone drops or tablets on hand, as the product can be somewhat effective for rabbits that have intestinal problems.

Sore Eyes

This is a common problem for baby rabbits in the first few weeks of life. As you know, kits are born "blind," with their eyes closed. Their eyes open at approximately nine to twelve days of

age. However, if a bacterial infection is present, the kits' eyes may literally be stuck shut. This may require some veterinary assistance, as you'll need to have the kits' eyes manually opened and then treat the infected eyes with an antibiotic ointment. Incidences of sore eyes can be decreased by making sure that the nest box area is kept as clean as possible. Unsanitary conditions are far more likely to result in sore eyes.

Hutch Burn

This can occur if your cages are not kept clean and dry. Hutch burn affects the genital areas, where you can see a visible burned appearance. The scalding is due to prolonged exposure to urine and can be caused by sitting on dirty, wet hay.

COPROPHAGY

You've just discovered your rabbit consuming his own feces. Why would he do this? Is he sick? The answer is no. Rabbits actually have a very good reason for practicing coprophagy (the consumption of feces). First, you need to understand that there are two types of droppings: the easily recognizable, typical rabbit droppings and "night feces." The latter are softer and look more like a tiny grape cluster; they also contain vitamins that are beneficial to a rabbit's digestion. Most rabbits consume their own night feces, and this is perfectly normal behavior. So, coprophagy in rabbits is something you simply don't need to worry about!

My, what small teeth you have! But if they don't align properly, your rabbit could face serious discomfort and even an inability to eat. Check your rabbit's teeth regularly.

An antibiotic ointment can be useful for treatment; ask your veterinarian's advice for selecting the proper type.

Malocclusion

While not exactly a medical issue (it isn't caused by illness or injury), malocclusion is a serious health issue affecting many rabbits. Malocclusion is also known as buck teeth or wolf teeth, and it is characterized by front teeth that do not meet properly. Rabbits' teeth continually grow, and if they are not worn down properly, they will become overgrown and may eventually become misaligned. This can cause the rabbit to

STOCKING YOUR BUNNY FIRST-AID KIT

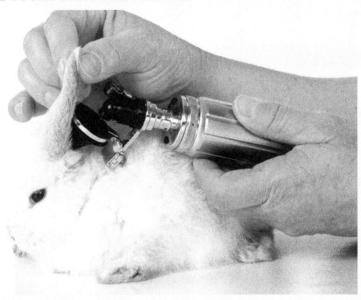

This list is not intended to replace medical advice, but only to give a guideline of items that you might wish to keep on hand as a rabbit owner:

- Nail clippers
- Teeth trimmers
- Cotton swabs or cotton balls
- Scissors (blunt-tipped safety scissors are a good choice)
- Disposable curve-tip syringes (without needles, useful for administering medication orally)
- Antibiotic ointment for treatment of sore eyes and hutch burn
- Ivomec (ivermectin dewormer)
- Mineral oil for treatment or prevention of ear canker
- Preparation H for treatment of sore hocks
- Simethicone drops or tablets for treatment of gastrointestinal problems
- Terramycin eye ointment for sore eyes
- Terramycin powder, if oral antibiotics are necessary

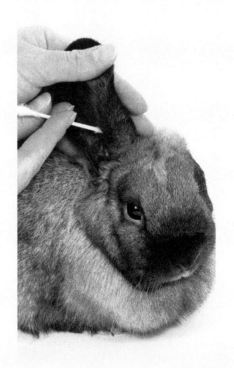

have difficulty eating and can also cause significant problems if the overgrown lower teeth begin protruding into the rabbit's nose or parts of its mouth. Teeth trimming is commonly recommended. Teeth trimmers can be purchased from rabbit supply companies. Again, I recommend that you seek the assistance of a veterinarian (or, at the very least, a longtime rabbit breeder) to help you with this task. Teeth trimming can have problematic results if you make a mistake, so be sure to have a knowledgeable person perform the task.

Red Urine

This can be a disturbing sight when you go to empty the trays under your rabbits' cages—reddish urine instead of the proper yellow/cream color that you're

Rabbits are, by nature, very tidy creatures. This Lionhead rabbit is washing his face and paws. *Shutterstock*

IMMUNIZATIONS

If you have other pets or livestock, you're probably aware of the fact that most animals need vaccinations to protect them (and you!) against various illnesses. Rabbits are the exception to this rule, as currently there are no vaccinations approved for use in rabbits.

used to seeing. Is it blood? If it is streaked with bright red, it could be blood and you should contact a vet immediately. But, if the color is actually a reddish brown, it is likely caused by nutrients that have failed to break down completely in the rabbit's digestive system, subsequently discoloring the urine. This is a harmless condition and requires no treatment. It typically resolves itself within a few days, but it is something that you should be aware of, if only to avoid unnecessary worrying.

Finding a Veterinarian

The time to locate a good veterinarian is *before* you need one. Don't wait until you have a sick or injured bunny before researching sources of veterinary assistance in your area. Small-animal

The time to locate a good veterinarian is *before* you need one. Don't wait until you have a sick or injured bunny before researching sources of veterinary assistance in your area.

veterinarians will usually treat rabbits—though not all will consider rabbits to be an area of expertise. *Rabbits USA* magazine, published annually by BowTie, Inc., provides a thorough listing of rabbit-friendly veterinarians, organized by state. This could be a good resource for you in locating a vet. Another good idea is to ask the advice of other local rabbit breeders or members of your 4-H or FFA club. See if they have any recommendations for veterinary care in your area.

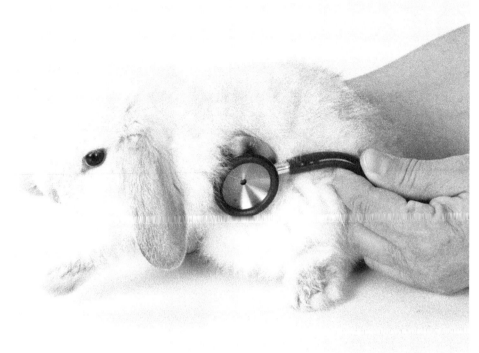

Not all veterinarians are willing to treat rabbits, and not all who are willing are truly knowledgeable about the unique aspects of medical treatment for rabbits. If you can find a rabbit-savvy veterinarian, you're very fortunate.

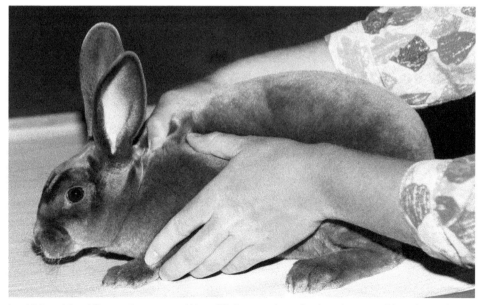

In addition, giving daily attention to your rabbits will help you to immediately notice any problems that might be brewing.

CHAPTER 6

Off to the Shows!

As cute as a button! But cuteness alone will not be enough for a rabbit to place well at a show. He will need to exhibit quality and breed type.

I t's show time! If you've ever thought about taking your rabbits to an American Rabbit Breeders Association (ARBA) or county fair show, this is the chapter for you. You'll find information on selecting and conditioning show rabbits, preparing for a show, and much more.

Selecting Show Rabbits

Although I've mentioned this already, I'm going to repeat myself: if you're serious about breeding or showing your rabbits, then it's vital for you to purchase a copy of the ARBA's *Standard of Perfection*.

This is the book that outlines the ideal standard for each and every one of the forty-seven breeds recognized by the ARBA; these standards are the criteria upon which rabbits are judged at shows. Therefore, by familiarizing yourself with

A young senior rabbit between eight and twelve months old is at a very good age to be shown competitively.

the standard for your rabbits' breed(s), you can get a fairly good idea of which of your rabbits would be the most likely candidates for showing.

Age is another consideration when selecting show specimens. If you want to be optimally competitive in the junior divisions, you'll want your youngsters to be as close as possible to six months of age on show day (without going over!). Similarly, if you're showing a breed with a 6/8 class (for more information on 6/8 classes, see "Four- and Six-Class Breeds," pages 109–110), it helps if your rabbits are nearly eight months, rather than just over six months.

In the senior divisions, your main consideration is to make sure that your show rabbits are not too old. Unfortunately, age does take its toll on rabbits, and they are markedly less competitive as they age. Many people believe that age two is about the maximum for showing competitively. Does that have raised litters may also be less competitive, although this is certainly not always the case.

Some shows offer pre-junior divisions for rabbits under three months of age, but you wouldn't want to exhibit any rabbits younger than eight weeks old; ten is better.

Obviously, you want your show rabbits to be in tiptop condition; this means that the rabbits must be in excellent health. Never show a rabbit that is not perfectly healthy. Shows can be stressful for rabbits, and you wouldn't want to compromise your rabbit's health by showing a sick animal. Additionally, consider the other exhibitors and their rabbits; it would be truly wrong to expose their animals to any type of communicable disease. Bottom line: if your rabbits are ill, keep them home.

SHOW TYPES

Show rabbits fall into three general categories:

- **Fancy** rabbits are the true exhibition breeds, bred for their beauty, including the popular Netherland Dwarf, Mini Rex, Holland Lop, Mini Lop, Polish, and Dutch.
- **Wool** rabbits are bred for their gorgeous coats of Angora fiber.
- **Commercial** rabbits are the meat breeds, including New Zealand Whites, Californians, and Florida Whites. These rabbits are judged on their conformity to meat type and flesh condition.

Conditioning

Rabbits rarely stay in a stagnant state of condition—they can (and do!) change frequently. This is especially true of junior rabbits, which are growing and changing. You might look at one of your junior rabbits one day and think, "Oh dear, she's not in good condition at all. Look at how her backbone shows, and her flesh is flabby." You might decide to increase her daily rations, or you might add a supplement or two. Or perhaps you might decide just to wait and see. A couple of weeks later, she may look entirely different: better weight, tighter flesh, a blooming coat.

There is much more to a rabbit's condition than simply being in good weight, although this is important. The condition of a rabbit's fur is another important facet; molting rabbits should not be exhibited at a show, regardless of how nice they are otherwise. Additionally, you may notice that sometimes your rabbits will seem a bit more "bloomy" than

Evaluate your rabbit's condition before deciding whether or not to enter him in a show. Good weight, good fur condition, and good firm flesh are some of the characteristics that you're seeking.

Feel along your rabbit's backbone; is it easily felt or well covered with fat?

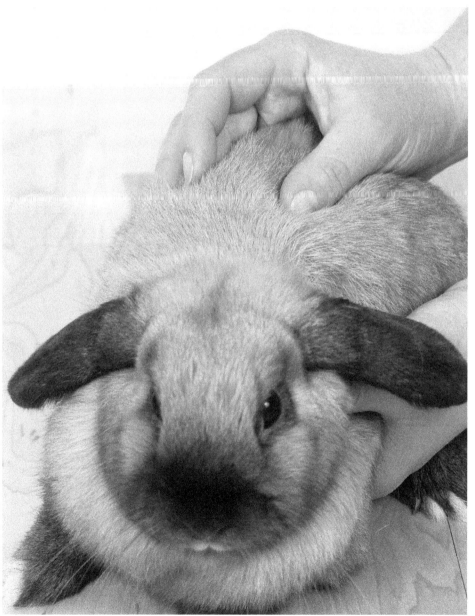

they do at other times. Coat condition can be cyclical in nature, and you might want to wait to show a particular rabbit until his or her coat improves.

However, weight and fur aside, you must pay attention to flesh firmness. This might seem a little abstract at first, but once you have observed the differences between firm flesh and flabby flesh, you'll immediately understand why firm flesh is so important to a rabbit's condition. Ask an experienced rabbit breeder or exhibitor to show you examples of a nicely conditioned animal in firm flesh, and examples of animals that are not. The visual and hands-on experience cannot be easily replicated in text. If you don't have a rabbit mentor to ask, see if someone at a show would be willing to help you.

Planning Ahead

Let's say that you have a national breed show convention that you want to attend at the end of April. Perhaps your goal is to show three promising junior rabbits at the April convention. In order to meet that goal, you're going to need to plan well in advance.

To be most competitive, you'll want your juniors to be as close as possible to six months old on show day, without being over. This means that you'll want your babies to turn six months old on May 1. Counting backward, this means that they will need to be born about November 1. To achieve this, you'll need to breed your parent stock on October 1. In the event of a missed pregnancy, you can always try again to breed in November and hope for almost-five-month-old babies in time for your April show. The point is that achieving a crop of promising juniors for a particular show takes time, effort, and advance planning.

It's wise to keep a calendar dedicated to your rabbit events. You can add all the dates of shows and fairs and easily keep track of future events.

ARBA Shows

There are approximately three thousand ARBA-sanctioned shows held in the United States each year. Chances are you'll be able to find one in your general vicinity; check out the ARBA's website (www.arba.net) for a calendar of shows.

As you begin looking at the show listings, you'll probably send away for information on a few of the shows that are closest to your home. You may find that some of the terminology is a bit confusing at first. What's a coop show? What's a carry cage show? And what's the difference?

Never fear, the answers are quite simple. Coop shows are typically larger-scale shows that extend over a period of at least two days. (The ARBA National Convention is a good example of a coop show.) Cages, also known as coops, are provided for the rabbits so that they do not have to stay in their carriers. In contrast, a carry cage show is shorter in duration (usually only one day) and cooping is not offered, so the rabbits are simply kept in their own personal travel carriers (or "carry cages") for the day.

A carry cage show is an ARBA show that is usually held in one day, so overnight cooping is not available. Instead, each rabbit spends the day in its own travel carrier.

Show Scheduling at ARBA Shows

Let's say that you're showing a young male rabbit. He is a Netherland Dwarf, and his color is black otter. Your first class will be for Otter Colored Netherland Dwarf junior bucks. All entries for a particular class are brought to the judging table and are evaluated by the judge; the winner is then set aside while all of the other classes are completed.

If your buck is fortunate enough to win his class, then he will compete for Best of Variety (BOV) against the other first-place winners in the Otter classes: the senior buck, the senior doe, and the junior doe. One of these four will be awarded BOV, and one of the opposite sex will be awarded Best Opposite Sex of Variety (BOSV).

Let's say that your junior buck wins BOV. Now it's time for him to compete against BOV winners in the following color varieties: Sable Marten, Silver Marten, Smoke Pearl Marten, and Tan. All four of these varieties, along with Otter, belong in Group 4, which is Tan Pattern Varieties. The winner of this is named Best of Group (BOG). The Best of Group winner goes on to compete with the other BOG winners for Best of Breed (BOB). Again, the best rabbit of the opposite sex wins Best Opposite Sex of Breed (BOS).

Just for the fun of it, let's say that your little otter junior buck goes all the way to the top, and is awarded Best of Breed. Now he is eligible to compete with all of the other BOB winners from the show; considering the fact that there are forty-seven breeds recognized by the ARBA, he will be up against some stiff competition! The chosen winner is named Best in Show (BIS), a true honor and cause for lots of excitement!

An "all breed show" is a show in which all ARBA-recognized breeds are eligible to show. You may notice that the show bill will mention that some breeds are "sanctioned" as well, but don't let this confuse you: even if your breed isn't sanctioned at that particular show, you can still show your rabbit. It just means that the sanctioned breeds can receive sweepstakes points, which are points that are tabulated by official ARBA breed specialty clubs. An all breed show is open to all breeds.

All About Legs

It's always exciting when your rabbit earns a "leg." Now, if you aren't familiar with the term, you might be scratching your head and asking, "How in the world does a rabbit 'earn' a leg?" The answer is quite simple: by winning at ARBA shows! Generally speaking, a rabbit with three "legs" is eligible to be "granded," which means that they have earned a Grand Championship title.

In order to earn a leg, your rabbit must place first in a class with at least five entries. Additionally, these five entries must be the property of at least three different exhibitors. (This means that you can't bring five rabbits of your own for a particular class and compete

When the time is nearing for your breed to be judged, you'll want to move your carriers closer to the judging area.

against only yourself to win a leg for one of your rabbits.) Legs can also be earned by winning Best of Group, Best of Variety, and of course Best in Show. "Granding" your rabbits is an excellent way of proving your stock and promoting your rabbitry.

Four- and Six-Class Breeds

Some rabbit breeds are shown as Four-Class breeds, while others are shown as Six-Class breeds. It's easy to determine which breeds belong in each classification. Any breed with an ideal senior weight of under nine pounds is a Four-Class breed, and any breed with an ideal senior weight of more than nine pounds is a Six-Class breed.

A Four-Class breed has four class divisions: senior buck, senior doe, junior buck, and junior doe. By this

Prizes are the icing on the cake at a rabbit show. In addition to winning trophies, your prize-winning rabbits can also earn "legs, which can in turn allow your rabbit to be "granded."

Rex rabbits, such as the one shown here, are a Four-Class breed, which means that they do not have additional classes for intermediate (six- to eight-month-old) rabbits.

MOST POPULAR AND LEAST POPULAR YOUTH BREEDS

The Netherland Dwarf is one of the most popular breeds with youth exhibitors.

Nearly 11,000 rabbits were exhibited at the 2009 ARBA National Convention in San Diego, California. Of these, more than 2,700 were shown by youth exhibitors. At the 2008 ARBA National Convention in Louisville, Kentucky, there were more than 5,700 rabbits shown by youth exhibitors. It is interesting to examine the list of the most popular breeds shown by youth, as it offers insight into the breeds that are most commonly preferred.

- Netherland Dwarf: 332 shown in 2009, 546 shown in 2008
- Mini Rex: 309 shown in 2009, 796 shown in 2008
- Holland Lop: 253 shown in 2009, 412 shown in 2008
- Mini Lop: 230 shown in 2009, 304 shown in 2008
- Polish: 193 shown in 2009, 261 shown in 2008
- Dutch: 176 shown in 2009, 346 shown in 2008

It's interesting to note that all of these breeds are under 6.5 pounds; most are under 5 pounds. This is a definite testament to the popularity of small breeds today: they are easy to handle, require less cage space and feed, and produce less manure.

Now, if going with the popular crowd isn't your cup of tea, then you might want to take a look at the following list of the *least* common breeds shown by youth exhibitors at recent conventions. If you begin raising and showing one of these breeds, you'll be helping to increase awareness about a lesser-known breed, and you won't have much in the way of competition. (You may see this as a positive aspect or a negative one, but either way it's true).

The less-common show breeds for youth are:

- Giant Angora: None shown at the 2008 or 2009 ARBA conventions
- Silver Fox: 3 shown in 2009, 37 shown in 2008
- Giant Chinchilla: 4 shown in 2009, 2 shown in 2008
- Standard Chinchilla: 4 shown in 2009, 17 shown in 2008
- Blanc de Hotot: 5 shown in 2009, 4 shown in 2008
- American Chinchilla: 6 shown in 2009, 4 shown in 2008
- Belgian Hare: 6 shown in 2009, 15 shown in 2008
- Checkered Giant: 6 shown in 2009, 22 shown in 2008
- Cinnamon: 7 shown in 2009, 25 shown in 2008
- English Angora: 7 shown in 2009, 21 shown in 2008
- Lilac: 7 shown in 2009, 26 shown in 2008
- Satin Angora: 7 shown in 2009, 1 shown in 2008
- Harlequin: 9 shown in 2009, 28 shown in 2008
- Beveren: 10 shown in 2009, 0 shown in 2008
- French Angora: 11 shown in 2009, 4 shown in 2008
- American: 13 shown in 2009, 6 shown in 2008
- Silver: 14 shown in 2009, 9 shown in 2008
- Rhinelander: 22 shown in 2009, 8 shown in 2008

Keep in mind that there may be reasons why some of these breeds are less popular, such as the intensive grooming needed for Angoras or the high feed costs of the giant breeds. Still, you may find that they are the most rewarding breed for you.

Fair shows have one major difference from ARBA shows: they often last considerably longer.

---

categorization, juniors are under six months old and seniors are over six months old.

A Six-Class breed breaks out the classes into six divisions: senior buck, senior doe, intermediate buck, intermediate doe, junior buck, and junior doe. By this categorization, intermediates are six to eight months of age (also known as 6/8s), and seniors are rabbits over eight months old.

4-H, FFA, and County Fair Shows

Fair shows have one major difference from ARBA shows: they often last considerably longer. An ARBA show lasts one or two days, while fairs typically require you to keep your entries at the show for the duration of the fair—often four days, or as long as a week. The fair rabbit show itself might only be a morning or a day, but you will probably be required to exhibit your rabbits on the premises for the entire fair. This can be a bit of extra effort for you, as you will need to attend the fair each day to care for your rabbits.

There are many benefits to fair shows, including greater exposure for your rabbits and your project. Think of the thousands of fairgoers who will be introduced to the wonders of rabbits and the enjoyment of their beauty!

County fair rabbit shows vary widely. Some offer only a couple of rabbit classes, while others offer a full-fledged ARBA-sanctioned all breed show. At my local county fair, classes are offered for breeds that are typically shown in this area. For

Exhibiting rabbits at your county fair can be a wonderful experience; take the time to truly enjoy the event!

New Zealands; if someone wanted to show a New Zealand Black, it would have to be shown in class G, "Any Other Commercial Breed."

Other county fairs might offer fewer classes. Some provide three classes only: Commercial, Fancy, and Wool. Others will offer those three categories along with individualized classes within each category. For instance, in the Commercial group, there might be classes for Grades, Californians, New Zealands, French Lops, and Other Purebred Commercial Breeds.

Additionally, county fairs often offer clases for meat pens, single fryers, and fancy threes (similar to a meat pen class, but for fancy breeds). These are in addition to the showmanship classes that give you the chance to show your skill in handling your rabbit, including carrying your rabbit; checking his teeth; examining his eyes, ears, and feet; and posing.

Many fair shows do not officially disqualify rabbits based on weight or breed standards as so often occurs at ARBA shows. Instead, the rabbit with the disqualification is placed last in the class.

Owning Bunnies

Let's say that it's early July, and Agatha has just purchased a new Mini Rex buck. He's a beautiful, show-quality rabbit, and he has an impressive pedigree of Grand Champions. Agatha can't wait to take him out to a show and see how he does on the show table.

Not so fast, Agatha.

Agatha's county fair is only a month away, and she would like to enter him in the 4-H show. However, the rules for

breeds without a specific class, "Any Other" classes are offered. For example:

A. New Zealand Whites
B. Flemish Giants (all colors)
C. Checkered Giants (all colors)
D. Dutch (all colors)
E. Chinchilla
F. Californian
G. Any Other Commercial Breed
H. Any Other Fancy Breed
I. French Lops
J. Holland Lops
K. Mini Lops
L. Jersey Wooly
M. Best Litter (any breed)

The breed classes are then divided into four groups: junior buck, junior doe, senior buck, and senior doe. The intermediate (6/8) classes are not offered.

Interestingly enough, even though Mini Rex rabbits are the most popular breed shown by youth exhibitors at ARBA conventions, you'll notice that there is no specific class for Mini Rex at my county fair. This is because we have far more Flemish Giants and New Zealand Whites in our area than we do Mini Rex. You'll also notice that class A is restricted to the White variety of

MEAT PEN PROJECT

The meat pen class is a popular one with youth exhibitors. To enter this class, you must enter three commercial rabbits of the same breed and variety. The maximum age for showing in a meat pen class is ten weeks, and the rabbits must weigh between three and five pounds; they usually do not need to come from the same litter. Your group of three rabbits is then evaluated on a point schedule, which allots 40 points for Meat Type, 30 points for Condition of Flesh, 20 points for Uniformity of Body and Weight, and 10 points for Fur. If any one of your three rabbits is found to have a DQ, then the entire group is disqualified.

The single fryer class is similar to a meat pen class, except that it requires only one rabbit instead of three. The same restrictions apply (up to ten weeks, three to five pounds); however, the point schedule for single fryers is slightly different than that of a meat pen. The point value for Meat Type is increased to 45 points, Condition of Flesh is increased to 35 points, and Fur is increased to 20 points.

Please keep in mind that these rules and points are as outlined by the ARBA; your local fair may work with slightly modified rules and regulations, so always check your fair book before entering.

A Californian rabbit.

her particular 4-H show require that all rabbits must be owned by the 4-H member as of May 15 of the current year. Agatha has only owned her Mini Rex for one week. She is ineligible to show him at that show.

The reasoning behind this is to make sure that the rabbits shown by 4-H members at their annual fair were actually raised by the 4-H members for a considerable period of time. Not that there's anything wrong with Agatha showing a rabbit that she recently purchased, but since she isn't the one responsible for his current state of condition or body weight, she truthfully can't take credit for him. This is why some 4-H shows place these restrictions on

County fairs might not offer classes for every single breed of rabbit, so you may have to enter yours in an "Any Other" type of category.

In order to show rabbits at most 4-H shows, you'll need to be the one handling the daily care of your rabbits.

entries—to ensure that the rabbits are the product of the 4-H member's care.

Another way for fairs to prove the length of ownership is to require pre-entries a couple of months prior to the date of the fair. This can be difficult for you, because it requires you to select your show rabbits far in advance. This is not always an easy task, since you can't predict

WHOSE BUNNY IS IT?

One thing to remember: when you are exhibiting your rabbits at a meat pen show or fair, you will probably be given exhibition tags for each entry. These are usually affixed to each rabbit's cage, allowing the show secretary to keep track of which entry is which. While you may be required to list your name and town or city on the entry tag, you should not place any other contact information (such as your address or phone number) on this tag. Consider the vast number of visitors that attend a county fair. Not all of these people are ones with whom you would want to share your address and phone number. So it's wise not to plaster your cages with easily visible contact information.

when a rabbit is going to molt or otherwise render himself unshowable. However, the early pre-entry date provides the show with the proof that you've been the one raising the rabbits for several months.

On the other hand, Agatha could take her brand-new buck to an ARBA-sanctioned show immediately and show him without any difficulties whatsoever.

This is because rabbits at ARBA shows are judged exclusively against the breed's standard without considering who might have provided the care.

Mixed Breeds

Unlike ARBA shows, many county fair shows require proof of pedigree. Does this mean that you can show a

PEOPLE YOU WILL MEET AT SHOWS

The Judge. The person whose opinion stands between your rabbits and their placings! You might feel nervous around a judge, but don't be afraid. Judges are nearly always very helpful people who are more than willing to educate and share their knowledge whenever possible. You might be surprised at just how "human" a judge can be. Be respectful, always—but not intimidated.

The Show Superintendent. A very busy person with a million things to take care of. A rabbit show superintendent is the person to whom you will turn with questions about anything relating to show day. Chances are, the superintendent will either know the answer to your question or can tell you who will.

Show Secretary. The paperwork person. The secretary keeps track of entries and knows who is entered where and when they need to be there. Show secretaries are a major part of the smooth running of a show.

Breed Chairperson. Need help with a breed-specific question? This is the person to ask. Breed chairpeople are often members of the local branch of a breed specialty club.

Remark Takers. An important volunteer job and an educational one! A remark taker sits with the judge during the exhibition process and transcribes the remarks about each rabbit. Remark takers are a blessing to exhibitors who desire permanent records of their rabbits' evaluations. If you're showing multiple bunnies, it's not always possible to personally observe each and every class—and even if you did, it's not easy to remember all of the remarks after a full day of showing. Remark takers also transcribe the results of each class.

Registrars. At ARBA shows, a registrar will be set up to process registrations for the ARBA. If your rabbit is over six months of age (eight months for a 6/8 breed), you can present your rabbit for evaluation with a registrar. If your rabbit meets the fundamental requirements of the breed's standard, meets the senior weight requirements, and has no disqualifications, then the registrar may approve your rabbit for ARBA registration. A fee of six dollars is collected. After submission to the ARBA, you are sent a registration certificate for your rabbit by mail. This certificate lists the rabbit's name, pedigree, number, owner, weight, and any Grand Championships. Proving the quality of your stock via registration is a smart and inexpensive way to build credibility with your rabbit project. If a licensed registrar has deemed your stock suitable for registration, then this may make your litters slightly more valuable in the future, if you're planning to sell kits later on. The easy accessibility of a registrar at ARBA shows makes this a great way to have your rabbits registered.

Other Exhibitors. Your friends, your competitors, your archrivals (just kidding)! Of all the people at a show, the other exhibitors are the ones with whom you'll be spending the most time. You'll be sharing floor space, standing in line together for the lunch stand, chatting over rabbits, and waiting to be judged together. Make friends, and value those friendships. It is fun to gather together with others who enjoy the same hobby, and you would never want to let a competition spoil a friendship. No show placing—good or bad—is worth it.

mixed-breed rabbit at an ARBA show? The answer is no. ARBA shows are designed for purebred animals that will be compared to the *Standard of Perfection* for their breed. While pedigrees are not specifically required at ARBA shows, it is understood that the animals are expected to be purebreds, and indeed, if you want your entries to be competitive, they will need to closely match the breed's *Standard of Perfection*.

Disqualifications

The list of potential disqualifications (DQs) is quite long, and all DQs are clearly outlined in the *Standard of Perfection*. Some DQs are very

Judging is not an easy job! Be kind and courteous to the judges and try to learn all you can from their expertise.

Be on time! If you're not exactly sure when your rabbits will be judged, ask the show secretary.

RABBIT SHOW REMARK CARD
American Rabbit Breeders Association, Inc.

Ear No. _____ Coop No. _____ Entry No. _____ X

Exhibitor _____ X

Address _____ X

Show _____ Date _____ X

Breed _____ Variety _____ X

Buck   Doe   Sr.   6/8   Jr.   Pre Jr.   Fryer   Meat Pen   Fur   X

No. in Class _____ Award _____ No. Exhibitors _____

B.O.B.   B.O.S.   B.O.G.   B.O.S.G.   B.O.V.   B.O.S.V.

Best Sr.   Best 6/8   Best Jr.   Best Pre-Jr.

	VG	G	F	P			VG	G	F	P
Head					Condition					
Ears					Butterfly					
Crown					Eye Circles					
Bone					Cheek Spots					
Type					Ear Base					
Shoulders					Side Markings					
Midsection					Spine/Herringbone					
Hindquarters					Blaze					
Fur/Wool					Cheeks					
Sheen					Neck					
Density					Saddle					
Texture					Undercut					
Color					Stops					
Remarks										

This is an example of the form that is filled out by a remark taker at a show.

straightforward—cut and dry, so to speak—while others are considered more judgmental. Let's go over a few of the less judgmental DQs:

- **Weight**. If your rabbit does not meet the specific criteria for its breed and age, it will be DQ'd.
- **Neutering**. Neutered animals are disqualified from competition, as are males over six months of age that do not have both testicles descended. Any male rabbit with a split penis is also DQ'd.
- **Classification**. Animals are DQ'd if they are entered in the improper class for their breed, group, variety, or sex.

- **Eyes**. Improperly colored eyes, wall eyes, unmatched eyes, speckled eyes, spotted eyes, marbled eyes, or any rabbit exhibiting signs of conjunctivitis will be DQ'd.
- **Faults**. Malocclusion of the teeth is cause for DQ, as is being pigeon breasted.
- **Toenails**. These are very important. Rabbits can be DQ'd for having improperly colored toenails, mismatched toenails, missing toenails, or toenails that are too short. Additionally, white toenails are a DQ in all colored breeds and varieties (specifically including any Himalayan or Californian colored rabbits and any of the Pointed White varieties). For any white rabbits or broken varieties (this includes

There are lots of other exhibitors at rabbit shows, so always try to be considerate of everyone's space. Keep your carriers in a small area.

Your rabbits must meet the weight requirements for their breed, as outlined in the ARBA's *Standard of Perfection*. If a rabbit does not meet the requirements, it will be disqualified.

A tattoo that isn't legible—or a tattoo that is in the wrong ear—is cause for disqualification.

Dutch rabbits), white toenails are a requirement.

- **Color**. Rabbits can also be DQ'd for color—including ring definition, lack of shading, and improper undercolor.

Showing Checklist

You're off to a show! You've packed up your bunnies in their travel carriers, and you're ready to hit the road—or are you?

Before you hop in the car, take a minute to go over your show checklist:

- Do you have the correct rabbits? This may sound obvious, but it's important to make sure that you bring along the proper rabbits. You wouldn't want to inadvertently choose the wrong black Havana as you're loading your show carriers. It's easy to make a mistake when you have multiple rabbits of the same color and breed.

- Your rabbits are in their travel carriers, but have you brought along additional necessary equipment? You'll want a floor mat/resting board for each carrier compartment, and food and water cups for each rabbit (or a tiny water bottle for each, if that's your preference).

- Don't pack your feeders and water cups and then forget food and water! You'll

Remember to bring along water from home in a container. Rabbits can be upset by a change in water and might not be willing to drink the water that is available at a show facility.

SHOWMANSHIP CLASSES

If you're up for a challenge—and a lot of fun too—then don't miss out on entering the rabbit showmanship classes at your local county fair. Unlike the other classes for rabbits, which are judged on the rabbit's quality, breed type, and condition, showmanship classes are judged on your knowledge and ability, in addition to the appearance of your rabbit.

In a showmanship class, you demonstrate your ability to properly hold, carry, and pose your rabbit. Then you perform a series of examinations on the rabbit, checking its eyes, mouth, legs, toenails, and other body parts before answering any questions that the judge may ask. It helps to be well prepared, so study your ARBA *Standard of Perfection* and *Guide Book* beforehand. The judge will assign points based on your ability to meet all of the criteria necessary for the class, and your score will reflect the total points earned.

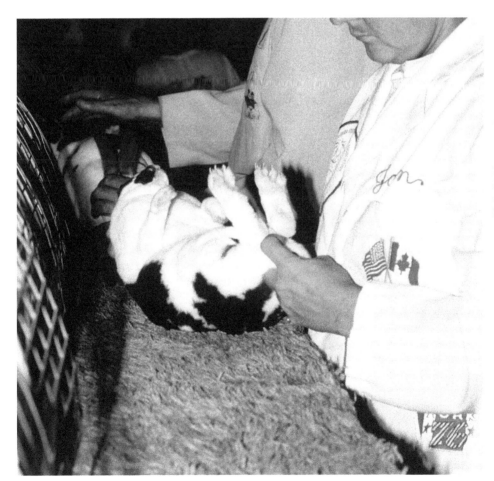

Carefully mark each of your rabbit carriers so that you can tell at a glance "who is who." You wouldn't want to accidentally present the wrong rabbit in the wrong class—a senior doe in a senior buck class, for instance.

want to bring along a sizeable portion of your rabbits' regular pellet feed, along with an ample supply of quality hay (rabbits will munch on hay while they travel in their carriers). Many people also bring along small pieces of white bread for their rabbits to enjoy while traveling. Also remember to bring along water from home in a container. Rabbits can be upset by a change in water and might not be willing to drink the water that is available at a show facility. Another option—albeit a more expensive one—would be to utilize commercially bottled water for your rabbits while traveling.

- Grooming supplies are important. This is show time, after all! Be sure to bring along your brushes, combs, scissors, nail clippers, waterless shampoo, and stain remover. Also be sure to bring your grooming apron!

- Don't forget a place to use those grooming supplies on your rabbits—so bring along a grooming stand, platform, or table. You'll want a safe and comfortable place to perform your grooming.

Judging Criteria

What is the most important characteristic in a show rabbit? A "typey" head that meets the exact description of the breed's standard? Ear length? Fur quality? Their pattern of markings? Body type?

The answers to these questions vary depending on the breed. Again, this is where the *Standard of Perfection* is going to help you. Each breed is judged upon a schedule of 100 points, which are clearly outlined in the book. For each breed, the 100 points are distributed differently, with varying amounts attributed to different characteristics. For instance, an English

Angora is allotted 57 points for wool and only 33 points for general type. The Holland Lop's schedule of points allots 84 points for general type and only 7 points for fur. However, on the Holland Lop, 42 of the 84 general type points are assigned to the head/ears/crown area. A New Zealand rabbit has 15 points for fur and 60 points for general type; only 5 of the general type points are assigned to the head and ears. So, as you can see, it's important to understand the primary characteristics upon which your breed is being judged, as the emphasis varies from breed to breed.

In addition to all of the physical breed characteristics that you'll want to be certain are present in your stock, you'll also want to select rabbits with good dispositions. You don't want rabbits that are bad tempered or biters.

TATTOOING AND POSING: TWO THINGS YOU NEED TO KNOW

Generally speaking, if you want to show your rabbit, it will need an identification tattoo in its left ear. All ARBA-sanctioned shows require this, and no rabbit is allowed to be shown without this identification. Imagine the situation: a class of sable point Netherland Dwarf senior does—all identical in color and similar in type. Without tattoos, confusion would reign.

Similarly, at most county fair shows, rabbits are usually required to be tattooed. There are exceptions to this, especially for "pet rabbit" classes, but otherwise tattoos are generally required.

For all types of shows, the rabbit's identification tattoo *must be in the left ear*. This is very important. This is where you place your personal identification tattoo for the rabbit. The ID system can be whatever and however you wish to identify your rabbits; you can even tattoo the rabbit's name, if desired. Rabbits with missing tattoos or identification tattoos in their right ear will be disqualified. The right ear is reserved for a tattoo of the rabbit's ARBA registration number, if it has one.

Aside from its importance with regard to showing, tattoos are beneficial for your own recordkeeping purposes. If you properly identify each rabbit with a permanent tattoo in its ear, you can avoid any confusion over which rabbit is which in your rabbitry.

There are a couple of different types of tattoo kits: the traditional "clamp style" tattoo and the newer "tattoo pen." The clamp-style tattoos generally produce clearer results, but the tattoo pens have the advantage of speed and ease. Regardless of the variety you choose, the resulting tattoo must be clearly defined in order to be easily read by judges and their staff. Tattoo kits are readily available from most rabbit equipment suppliers.

Another important part of the showing process is to have a clear understanding of posing. Rabbits are posed on the show table according to their shape. For instance, Full Arch rabbits are posed differently than Compact breeds, just as Cylindrical rabbits are posed differently than Semi-Arches (see Chapter 1, pages 18–19, for a complete breed list by shape). Therefore, your first step is to purchase a copy of the *Standard of Perfection*. This is a vital reference for your home library, regardless of whether you are showing at ARBA-sanctioned shows or at county fair shows. The *Standard* outlines the proper posing procedure for each rabbit shape, including special information for posing Netherland Dwarf and Holland Lop rabbits. If you work with your rabbits at home, then they will have a higher chance of posing properly for the judge during their class. Remember, in most classes (and always at ARBA shows), you will not be the one handling your rabbit on the show table. Only in 4-H showmanship classes will you be the one presenting your rabbit and handling the posing. So be sure that your bunny is familiar with the procedure of being posed ahead of time.

Here is an example of a clearly defined tattoo that is in the correct (left) ear.

Clamp-style tattoo kits are the traditional choice and generally work quite well.

HELP—MY RABBIT DIDN'T WIN!

It's disappointing. Of that, there is no question. Weeks—sometimes months!—of planning and preparation, not to mention the time spent traveling to and attending a show, and now you're back at home with a bunny that didn't win.

Now, chances are, you exhibited more than one rabbit at the show, so perhaps some of your other exhibits placed better. But let's say that you had one particular rabbit that you thought was exceptionally nice—and he placed eighth.

Ouch! Now what? Does this end his show career forever? Does it mean that he shouldn't be used for breeding? Does it mean that you should immediately sell him or give him away as a pet?

The simplest answer to these questions is to take a deep breath and not jump to any hasty conclusions. One show is simply that: one show and one judge's opinion. You should never let a single judge sway you to make any permanent decisions about your rabbitry and breeding program. If your rabbit meets your interpretation of his breed's *Standard of Perfection*, then don't assume that his show career is over. Take him out to another show and exhibit him under a different judge. You may be surprised by a better placing. Then again, he might not place well this time either. Then you must ask

yourself: is he in top condition? Perhaps his weight or coat condition is not up to par rather than there being a problem with his type. If you can improve his external appearance, you may find that he will place better on the show table.

If he has specific characteristics that you feel are important to your breeding program, then perhaps his value to you as a sire will diminish the importance of whether or not he is winning on the show table. Of course, we would all like our rabbits to win consistently, but sometimes there are other criteria that are also important.

Now, it's also true that a rabbit with a good show record (championships and legs) is very beneficial, especially in the early stages of your breeding program when you are trying to establish a reputation for high-quality stock. If you can prove your foundation stock through successful show results, you may find it easier to sell subsequent litters.

Then again, you might find that a particular rabbit consistently places poorly at shows, despite being in good condition. If judge after judge confirms that he is lacking in breed type or quality, *then* you might want to seriously consider the possibility of removing that particular bunny from your breeding program. He can certainly remain in your possession as a pet, or you might decide to find him a loving home where he will be enjoyed as a companion rabbit. These are decisions that only you can make.

Developing New Varieties

As any longtime rabbit breeder will tell you, developing new rabbit varieties is a time-consuming and lengthy process. They will also tell you that it is a satisfying and rewarding pursuit, despite the inevitable difficulties. Let's take a quick look at the process involved with developing a new variety. (Keep in mind that the process for developing a new breed is similar.)

Oliver has been raising Dutch rabbits for six years. He raises three varieties: black, blue, and chocolate. But what truly interests Oliver is the idea of raising lilac Dutch. Unfortunately, the lilac Dutch is not an ARBA-recognized variety. Since Oliver has been an ARBA member for more than five years, he is eligible to apply for a Certificate of Development (COD) from the ARBA. Oliver prepares a written standard for the lilac Dutch and submits it to the ARBA with an application fee.

Now let's say that the ARBA approves Oliver's request, and he is issued a COD for lilac Dutch. (For the purpose of this illustration, we'll assume that Oliver is the first person to request a COD for lilac Dutch. If other ARBA members have previously requested CODs for the same variety, their requests have precedence and Oliver's COD could only become active if the previous owners were to lose the rights to their CODs. But for this discussion, let's say that Oliver is first in line.) Oliver must now work on the development of this new variety for three years. After three years have passed, he can begin the process of officially presenting the new variety at three ARBA National Conventions. The ARBA allows a period of five years to achieve these three presentations. When Oliver exhibits specimens of his new lilac Dutch at the first ARBA National Convention, the Standards Committee evaluates his presentation and he is issued either a Pass or a Fail. If his presentation passes, he's allowed to try for his second presentation the following year; if his presentation fails, he goes back to step one and is

JUDGING YOUR OWN

New Zealand rabbit.

As you prepare for showing your rabbits in 4-H classes, it is a good idea to practice judging your own rabbits ahead of time. Not only will this help you to choose the best rabbits for exhibition, but it will also help you to articulate your thoughts and opinions about each rabbit.

Begin by selecting three or four of your rabbits to compare and evaluate. Open your *Standard of Perfection* and locate the section on the breed that you're evaluating. Let's say that you have a senior Dutch doe. Look at the schedule of points for a Dutch rabbit, and score your rabbit on each of the points listed. Examine her body, head, ears, eyes, fur, color, markings, and condition, in addition to checking for any DQs. Try to describe her positive qualities and her faults as you work. For instance: "This doe's head is not as round as I would like to see, although her eyes are bright and clear." Or: "Her cheek markings are excellent, but her saddle is a bit jagged."

Continue the process with each of your rabbits, then compare their scores when you're finished. It's one thing to think to yourself, "My New Zealand doe is a much better rabbit than my Mini Rex buck," but it's very helpful to truly evaluate the exact characteristics of each rabbit.

allowed to try once more to achieve his first successful presentation. If his second consecutive presentation fails, he loses his COD. If his first and second presentations pass, he is allowed to present for a third time. If the third presentation also passes, the new variety is accepted as an official variety of the breed.

Developing a new breed or variety requires a large measure of patience, a heavy dose of determination, and intense dedication.

The point scale for judging wool breeds places a higher emphasis on the fur quality than many of the fancy or commercial breeds. *Shutterstock*

Your First Litter

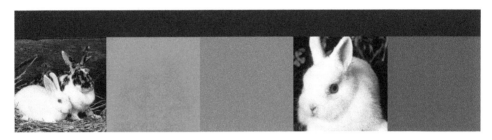

Raising a litter of baby rabbits is a very special time. Enjoy the delights of your kits!

Your first litter! This is an exciting time, and can be a little nerve-wracking as well. You want to be sure that all goes smoothly, and yet you don't want to spend the twenty-eight to thirty-three days of your doe's gestation in a fog of fear either. What to do? Sit back and take a deep breath: we'll walk you through it.

Things to Consider Before Breeding

Raising a litter of kits (baby rabbits) requires a lot of thought and is a definite commitment. There are several questions that you should ask yourself before raising a litter.

Are my buck and doe of the same breed?
Mixed-breed rabbits are not highly sought after, and they are usually unable

Although mixed-breed rabbits can be very cute—as shown here—the production of mixed-breed rabbits is generally discouraged. Always select two rabbits of the same breed when choosing a buck and a doe for breeding

to exhibit at shows. For this reason, we recommend that you only raise purebred stock, which means starting with purebred animals and only breeding rabbits of the same breed. You wouldn't want to breed a Jersey Wooly to a Mini Lop, for instance.

Are my rabbits quality examples of their breed?

They may not be grand champions, but your rabbits should essentially meet the criteria of quality as outlined in their breed's *Standard of Perfection* in order to be considered breeding stock.

Is this a convenient time for me to be managing a litter?

You'll be taking care of your newborn litter on a daily basis, so be aware that the average length of gestation (pregnancy) in rabbits is twenty-eight to thirty-three days. This means that before you breed your rabbits, double check your calendar. Don't schedule a litter to arrive if you have any upcoming vacations or other commitments that would prevent you from being available to care for your new litter. If you are heading away to summer camp for the first week of July, don't breed your rabbits in the first week of June.

Are you prepared for the commitment of raising baby rabbits? You'll be spending about three months raising your litter: one month of gestation and two months of raising the bunnies until weaning.

Do I have the space to raise a litter?

The baby rabbits will share a hutch with their mother for the first several weeks after birth, but what about after weaning? Do you have extra empty hutches for the babies once they are weaned? Remember, does can easily produce six kits in a single litter, and larger breeds regularly pop out ten or more kits at a time, so be prepared.

Breeding One Doe? Or Two?

As a first-time rabbit breeder, you might think it wise to breed a single buck to a single doe and raise one litter to get your feet wet. However, it's good practice to breed more than one doe at the same time. This is where the breeding trio (a buck and two does) comes in. This is helpful in several scenarios, and recommended by longtime breeders. The idea is that the kits could be fostered to the other doe, if need be.

Fostering comes into play if one of the does dies after kindling. In this unfortunate event, you will be able to foster the orphaned young to the other nursing doe.

Fostering is also an option if one of the does produces a small litter and the other delivers a large litter. Say one doe delivers a litter of two kits and the other delivers a litter of seven; you could foster a couple from the larger litter into the smaller litter. This equalizes the available milk supplies, as well as giving added warmth to the smaller litter. Kits rely on each other for body heat as they snuggle together in their nests.

Fostering is especially helpful when a doe produces only one surviving kit. There are a couple of problems with raising a litter of one. The single kit has a hard time generating enough body heat to sustain itself. This is not to say that single kits cannot survive on their own; they can and they do. It's just that if you have the option of adding a couple of foster siblings to a single kit's nest box, he will be much warmer and happier. Also, a single kit raised by a doe is

The condition of your breeding doe is important. She should be neither too thin nor overweight. Does that are overweight are at an increased risk of complications during pregnancy, including toxemia.

Don't overlook the importance of your breeding buck; top-quality breeding stock increases the chances of producing top-quality kits.

receiving all of the available milk and may become overweight too quickly, possibly overgrowing the preferred size for his breed.

One thing to remember when fostering: you must be able to identify the kits later on, in order to connect them with the proper pedigrees and parentage. This would be easy if you were fostering Mini Rex kits to an American Fuzzy Lop litter, or broken blue Mini Rexes to a litter of black Mini Rexes. But if you're working with a breeding trio of New Zealand Whites, it is much more complicated.

When it's time for breeding, take your chosen doe and carry her to the buck's cage. This is important. It is dangerous to bring the buck to the doe's cage; does are noted for being very territorial, and she may injure a buck in her cage.

Avoid any confusion by marking the interiors of the fostered kits' ears with a permanent marker or other identifying mark. Later on, you can separate the kits by their marks or lack thereof.

Fostering is a good option if you have more than one doe producing a litter at the same time. Always be sure that you can positively identify the kits in the future.

Mating Basics

When it's time for breeding, take your chosen doe and carry her to the buck's cage. **This is important**. It is dangerous to bring the buck to the doe's cage; does are noted for being very territorial, and she may injure a buck in her cage. So bring the doe and place her in the buck's cage. The mating usually takes place very quickly, and you'll probably be able to remove the doe from the cage within a few minutes. You can take the doe back to the buck again for another breeding later in the day (approximately eight to ten hours later, although some breeders feel that waiting four to six hours is sufficient). It is thought that a second breeding can increase the number of kits in each litter and that it can also increase the odds of achieving pregnancy. If larger litters aren't your ideal (some people do prefer smaller litters), then a single breeding might suffice.

Is She Pregnant?

After the breeding, what happens? You wait. It may seem like an interminable amount of time, but you'll have to wait

At eighteen days of gestation, this Dutch doe is carrying her breakfast hay around in her mouth. This nesting behavior is a good indicator of pregnancy.

A doe may occasionally experience a false pregnancy. This can occur regardless or whether she has been bred or not. This Holland Lop doe made a nest and pulled vast quantities of fur for a nest, but she wasn't pregnant. False pregnancies are not worrisome, just something that you should be aware of, especially if you keep only two pet does and are wondering what on earth is going on with all the nest building!

ten to fourteen days before you will have an idea of whether or not the breeding resulted in a successful pregnancy. At that time, pregnancy may be detected by means of palpation (externally massaging the doe's abdomen for the presence of growing kits); however, this should be performed by an experienced rabbit breeder. Find someone knowledgeable on the subject of palpation, and see if they would be willing to share their expertise with you. Palpation isn't particularly difficult if you know what you're doing—but if you don't, it can be a frustrating and potentially painful experience for you and your rabbit.

If the results of the palpation are positive, and there is a litter of kits on the way, then it's time to celebrate! If the palpation is negative, or inconclusive, the waiting game continues.

Many people will tell you that if a doe begins to make a nest within two weeks of her breeding date, then she is not pregnant. What they really mean is that if she begins to *pull fur* prior to approximately fourteen days of gestation, then she is probably experiencing a false pregnancy and will not produce a litter. However, if your doe is carrying hay around in her mouth or digging in the corners of her hutch, these are excellent signs that she is indeed pregnant, regardless of the date of her pregnancy.

Nest Boxes 101

On the twenty-sixth day after breeding, it's time to add a nest box to your doe's cage. You should do this regardless of whether you think the breeding was successful; you want to be prepared in any event.

There are several types of nest boxes available, or you can build your own. One commonly seen type is made of galvanized steel and has a removable floor, sometimes made of wood or Masonite, and usually with drainage holes. Other nest boxes are made entirely of wood. Wooden nest boxes should also have drainage holes, so many people use hardware cloth as a floor. This makes for easy cleaning and disinfecting after the litter has grown and exited the nest box. You can also find

A common type of nest box is made of galvanized steel with a removable floor that is made of perforated Masonite.

You can purchase prefabricated wooden nest boxes, or you can purchase wooden nest box kits (shown here), or you can make your own from scratch.

At thirty days of gestation, this doe is adding bits of hay to her new nest box.

nest boxes that are more basketlike in appearance. Others are designed to be inserted in the floor of the hutch, which requires cutting the wire on your cage

> You may be surprised by the volume of fur that your doe will pull out for her nest. It often looks as though a furball has exploded in the cage, especially when the fur is spread from corner to corner. This is normal; it means your doe is getting ready to be a good mother.

floor and eliminates the ability to use a tray under your cage.

The size of your nest box depends upon the size of your doe. Generally speaking, you want your nest boxes to be only slightly larger than your doe. You don't want your nest box to be too large; if it is, the babies may not stay huddled together as well.

If your nest box has a wire floor, you'll want to add a protective layer of cardboard to the bottom of the box. You may want to go ahead and add the

And here they are! Newly arrived kits, just an hour old, rest comfortably in their nest. Note how they huddle together for warmth.

cardboard even if the floor is made of steel, wood, or Masonite; the added layer of protection helps to keep your kits warm. On top of the cardboard, you can add a layer of wood shavings (a couple of inches deep), as this will help to keep the nest box dry. At this point, you can fill the nest box with hay if you like, or you can place the empty nest box in your doe's cage and supply her with extra hay outside of the nest box. This way, she can build her nest exactly as she pleases. As the date of delivery approaches, your doe will begin to pull fur from her belly to add to her nest. This fur provides an excellent layer of warmth for the newborn kits.

You may be surprised by the volume of fur that your doe will pull out for her nest. It often looks as though a furball has exploded in the cage, especially when the fur is spread from corner to corner. This is normal; it means your doe is getting ready to be a good mother.

Kindling Time

The birthing of rabbits is known as kindling. Now that it's the twenty-eighth, or twenty-ninth, or thirtieth day after breeding, you're beginning to get impatient. Just when are those kits going to arrive, anyway? While it's understandable to be anxious for the safe arrival of your new litter, it's important to give your doe as much peace and quiet as you can. Does can become nervous around kindling, and you want to make her environment as peaceful as you can. Avoid loud or unfamiliar noises, and try and keep visitors to a minimum.

At the same time, quietly pay attention to your doe. While you will probably not see her delivering her kits, you will want to notice as soon as they've arrived. If all of the kits are safely tucked into the nest box, then you can breathe a sigh of relief. If they're not—for instance, if they are scattered around the hutch—then you will want to gather them together and place them in the nest yourself. Kits must have the warmth of each other and the nest in order to survive, and they simply cannot if they are by themselves on the cold wire floor of a hutch.

In the Nursery

All right, the kits have arrived. They are safely tucked into their nest box, and your doe is alert, happy, and hungry. Now what?

At least once a day, you will want to check on the kits in the nest box. Many people mistakenly believe that kits cannot be handled or else the doe will reject them. However, it's important to check your nest box on a regular basis.

CUTTING BACK

Reduce your doe's ration of pellets during the last couple of days of her pregnancy, then gradually begin to increase her feed again after her litter is a couple of days old. The reduction of feed is designed to reduce the doe's risk of developing "caked breast," which is an overengorgement of milk and can develop into mastitis. Reduced feed intake can help to avoid these problems.

CHAPTER 7

SAVING A BABY

Most of the time, does deliver their kits safely and without incident. Occasionally, however, there can be problems. If your doe has delivered a litter and one or more of the kits are chilled, it's possible that you can save it by carefully warming its body temperature. This is accomplished in a couple of ways. You can bring the kit indoors and carefully blow it with a hair dryer. Another method is to run warm water over the kit's body (not its head, for obvious reasons) until its body temperature rises. You have two main objectives in this situation: to help the kit survive by bringing its body temperature up, and not to burn or scald the kit in the process. Many kits have been saved by the quick action of a heroic human—so keep these tricks in mind and you just might save a kit of your own someday.

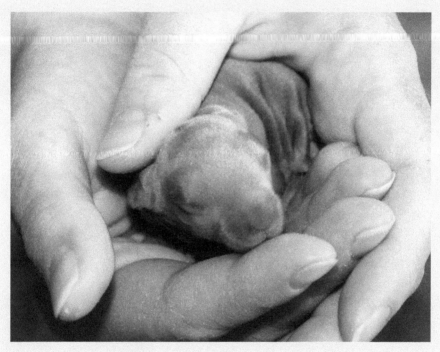

If you find a newborn baby kit that is out of its nest box but still alive, you'll need to warm it up immediately. If it is allowed to become chilled, it will likely die.

Sadly, not all kits survive the first two weeks after birth, so you need to check each day to make sure that all of the kits are alive and thriving. Ideally, you want to see a nice, round, full belly on each baby. This means that the kit is nursing. (Does only nurse their young once or twice per day, so don't worry if you don't actually observe her nursing the babies. Just watch for those round bellies.) If you find that a kit has died, remove it from the nest box immediately. If you notice

At a few days old, a baby rabbit is virtually furless and its eyes are closed.

that one or more of the kits isn't thriving as well as the others, you may want to assist the kit with nursing. This involves restraining your doe and guiding the kit underneath the doe until it finds a teat and is able to nurse. You may need to do this twice a day until the kit grows stronger. You don't want to handle the kits any more than necessary (remember, they need to stay warm within the nest box), but don't be afraid to handle them if you have to.

On or around the ninth day after kindling, the time has come to clean the nest box. Remove the box from your doe's hutch and carefully transfer the babies to a safe location. Empty the nest box of its contents—soiled hay, droppings, urine, and fur—and then replenish the nest with fresh hay bedding. Once you've re-bedded the box, transfer the babies back into it and replace the box in the doe's hutch.

Watching Your Babies

Baby rabbits are born with their eyes closed, and their eyes do not open until the kits are about ten days of age. In the meantime, the litter is supposed to stay safely tucked inside the nest box. It's important that they are kept in a safe environment.

However, just because the babies are *supposed* to stay in their nest box doesn't necessarily mean that they *will* stay in their nest box. Sometimes babies manage to crawl out of the box, and sometimes one is inadvertently carried out of the box by the doe after she nurses (if the

YOUR FIRST LITTER

Ready to explore! At three weeks old, this Rex kit is out of the nest box and ready to take on the world.

baby neglects to let go). In any case, if you discover that a kit has escaped into the cage, be sure to promptly return him to his nest.

On the typical wire hutch or cage, it's remotely possible for a newborn kit to crawl out of the nest box and through the wire out of the cage. This is a scenario that you want to avoid at all costs. You can purchase "baby saver wire" (with smaller openings than traditional cage wire) to place on the lower portions of your cage walls; alternately, urine guards would achieve the same effect. I've had success using snap-on resting boards, placed on the walls instead of on the floor of the cage. Once the babies are large enough, you can remove these baby guards, if desired.

By two or three weeks, your litter will be quite a bit more active, and once their eyes are open—look out! Babies love to play, and you'll undoubtedly spend many enjoyable times watching their adorable antics.

Feeding Requirements

Your doe requires considerably more food and water while nursing than when she is not. Because she is supporting a growing litter, her own dietary needs increase, and you will want to be vigilant about making sure that she has continuous access to fresh, clean water. Keep plenty of hay in front of her, and slowly increase her daily ration of pellets until she's getting as much as she can eat in a twenty-four-hour period. Additionally, once the litter has exited the nest box and begins eating along with her, the amount of pellets that you need to feed will increase again.

At weaning time, gradually remove the kits, leaving the smallest kit or two with the doe for a few extra days.

Weaning

The theories on weaning vary from breeder to breeder. Some breeders wean their litters at four weeks; however, this is typically done when the rabbits are being raised commercially and the does are scheduled to produce multiple litters per year. You don't need to do this in your home rabbit project. Instead, you can afford to let your litters stay with their mothers for six to eight weeks, depending on the condition of both mom and babies. When it is time to begin the weaning process, don't deprive the doe of all of her babies at once. Select the largest, chubbiest babies (no more than two), and remove them to a new hutch. Leave the doe with her remaining babies for a few more days. Repeat the process with another kit or two, until she is left with only one—the smallest. After another few days, that baby can be weaned as well.

Things to Watch For

After weaning, and even during the weaning process, watch your doe closely for any signs of mastitis (see pages 93–94). This is an infection of the mammary glands. Signs of mastitis include teats that are hot and swollen. This illness requires medical treatment and antibiotics; check your does regularly so that you don't accidentally miss it.

Another thing to watch for is the health of your newly weaned babies. Weanling rabbits are at increased risk of mucoid enteritis, a digestive problem (see pages 94–95). You can take steps to minimize their risk of this problem by giving them access to lots of hay and withholding any greens, fruits, or vegetables until they are over six months old. Mucoid enteritis is characterized by diarrhea, lethargy, and failure to thrive; a potbellied appearance can be another signal.

At weaning time, separate the young rabbits by gender. For a few more weeks, you can usually house your baby bucks together in one hutch and your baby does in another, but this probably will not work for a long period of time. Young bucks often begin fighting with one another, and young does can become a bit territorial as well, so keep an eye out for fighting and separate the babies further as needed.

Parting with Your Babies

This is the part of raising rabbits that can be a little tough, especially the first time

Vigilantly watch your baby rabbits for signs of mucoid enteritis, including diarrhea, lethargy, and a lack of growth.

you raise a litter. Let's say there are six kits in the litter. Chances are that's more than you'll be able to keep yourself. You may decide to keep three—two does and one promising buck—but that still leaves three other kits. You may decide to offer these for sale.

At first, it might seem hard to think about parting with some of the babies that you've raised yourself. You've watched them grow, watched them play, nurtured them, and brought them up, and now it's time to sell them. But if you're serious about raising rabbits, you must remain focused on your goals. If you want to raise the very best rabbits for show, then you will want to carefully select and keep only the top, show-quality kits. This means that you won't be able to keep every kit from every litter. The lower-quality kits won't be beneficial to your future breeding program, but that doesn't mean that they wouldn't make excellent pets for someone else, so consider selling them as pet bunnies to local families. The joy that your bunnies will be bringing to young children and their families can help to ease the pain of parting with your rabbits. If you know they are in good homes, well loved, and cared for, it will definitely be easier.

Round Two: Rebreeding Your Doe

Your first litter is beautiful; the babies are of excellent type and quality. The litter is six weeks old, and you're planning to begin the weaning process shortly. Is this a good time to rebreed your doe for a second litter?

Babies are endearing and adorable—and it can be hard to imagine selling them, but it's not practical to assume that you'll have the space to keep them all.

Be careful! Handle your kits gently and kindly, taking care not to drop them (they can be very squirmy!).

It could be, but first you will want to carefully evaluate your doe's condition. Take her out of her hutch and examine her. Is she in good weight? Or has nursing her litter pulled down her condition? How is her coat? Is it shiny and lustrous—or is she molting? If she is in good weight and condition, and you have the cage space to house the projected litter, then you could certainly make the choice to raise a second litter. On the other hand, you might want to give your doe another few weeks of rest, and select a different doe to breed. There are many options.

You can learn a lot simply by watching your doe interact with her young. Don't underestimate the importance of the maternal bond. I once had a doe that would make whimpering noises when I removed her nest box to check on her babies. *Shutterstock*

KEEPING RECORDS

You might think that recordkeeping is something that's only for large rabbitries, but it's very important for you to keep accurate and detailed records of your rabbit project. Let's compare two scenarios as an example.

Bev has twelve rabbits, all Florida Whites. Some of them were already tattooed when Bev purchased them. Since then, her does have produced a couple of litters, and Bev kind of mixed the litters up when she weaned them. Now she isn't sure which offspring came from which doe, and since they all look the same, things have gotten a bit confusing. Because of this, she can't produce pedigrees for the litters, even though the parent stock is pedigreed. Bev recently rebred both does, about a week apart, and she didn't write down the breeding dates. Now she can't remember which doe is due first or which buck she bred each one to. Bev's rabbitry is a confused mess due to a lack of recordkeeping.

Violet also has twelve Florida White rabbits, but careful recordkeeping is very important to Violet. When her litters are a couple of weeks old, Violet identifies each kit with a temporary ear mark that indicates which litter it came from. Her thorough breeding records allow her to produce accurate pedigrees for her youngsters when the time comes to sell them. Later, Violet tattoos each kit with a permanent mark that will identify them forever. Because Violet keeps detailed breeding records, she is easily able to calculate the exact dates that her does are due to kindle; this also allows Violet to palpate her does at ten to twelve days of gestation in order to determine whether or not they are pregnant.

The moral of the story? Be like Violet. Keep records.

Now, your recordkeeping doesn't have to be anything fancy. You can keep your records on a computer if you like, but a notebook works perfectly well. You will want to keep track of the breeding dates for all does, the projected palpation date, and the due date, and then record the actual date of the kits' arrival. This will help you to determine when it's time to wean the babies and also the best time to rebreed your does. Keep track of how many kits per litter and how many survived, and prepare an identification number for each kit so that they are permanently identified. You can tattoo each kit later on with this number, and you can cross-reference back to your records to prepare pedigrees when it's time to show or sell the rabbits.

Space

As a youth breeder, you may be dealing with an issue that isn't always a problem for adult rabbit enthusiasts: limited space. An adult can more or less choose the number of rabbits that they wish to keep; if they have space and are so inclined, they can set up a fifty-hole rabbitry and raise bunnies to their heart's content. You may not have that luxury.

For instance, you may wish to keep your rabbits in your parents' garage.

That may be fine and dandy—*if* you only have a few rabbits. Six or eight might be manageable and not overwhelming to your shared space. Keeping forty rabbits in your parents' garage will probably not be as workable.

Another consideration is the expense. You may be raising your rabbits on a very small budget, in which case you will almost certainly need to keep your numbers low in order to be able to afford equipment, hutches, feed, hay,

In addition, show records are also very valuable to have, so take the time to permanently record the results of your rabbits' placings at shows. You can subsequently add the show information to your rabbits' pedigrees.

An organized rabbitry means organized records. Take this seriously.

Variety **CHESTNUT**

Date of Birth: **5/04/2007**   Sex **DOE**
Registration Weight: **3.08**

DATE REGISTERED _3/20/2008_   ENTERED _4/21/2008_

Registration Merit Status
RED

SIRE
Name/Ear#: CRYSTAL'S BLANC 84W5
Reg#: R515F   Wt: 3.12   GC#: M 1
Variety: REW

DAM
Name/Ear#: MCKIE'S KAYLEE KL
Reg#: **R142E**   Wt: 3.06   GC#:
Variety: BKN BLACK

Original Breeder

G SIRE
Name/Ear#: OSWALD'S ACE 19
Reg#: **L302A**   WT: 3.08   GC#: **W2003**
Variety: BLUE OTTER

G DAM
Name/Ear#: MCKIE'S BWR HM03
Wt: 3.12
Variety: REW

G SIRE
Name/Ear#: MCKIE'S KINOBE C1
Wt: 2.12
Variety: BKN BLACK

G DAM
Name/Ear#: COY'S COBALT BLUE JD
Wt: 3.06
Variety: BLUE

GG SIRE
Name/Ear#: CAUDILL'S LITTLE REW JZ
Reg#: **M794B**   Wt: 3.00   GC#:
Variety: REW

GG DAM
Name/Ear#: HAWKINS' BUBBLES X4
Wt: 3.00
Variety: BLUE OTTER

GG SIRE
Name/Ear#: MCKIE'S BOB WHITE BS
Reg#: **Z77B**   Wt: 3.00   GC#: **W714**
Variety: REW

GG DAM
Name/Ear#: MCKIE'S ROZIE RP
Reg#: **L290A**   Wt: 2.12   GC#:
Variety: CHESTNUT

GG SIRE
Name/Ear#: MCKIE'S QB1
Wt: 3.02
Variety: BKN BLACK OTTER

GG DAM
Name/Ear#: MCKIE'S CHICKLETT CS
Wt: 3.04
Variety: REW

GG SIRE
Name/Ear#: COY'S DARICK R1
Reg#: **E449B**   Wt: 3.04   GC#: **T3325**
Variety: REW

GG DAM

and all of the other items necessary for proper rabbit care. Generally, rabbits are not expensive to keep, but they do need to be housed and fed, and the costs of keeping large numbers of rabbits can really add up.

All of this may be perfectly fine with you. Perhaps you don't feel prepared to care for more than half a dozen rabbits anyway. But if you have any desire to work on a long-term rabbit project (developing a new breed or variety, for example, or raising top-notch fancy show rabbits), you may discover that you simply don't have the space or budget to pursue these goals.

Don't let this discourage you. Getting started—small—when you are young is one of the best ways to educate yourself in the world of rabbits, and you can learn an amazing number of skills while keeping only a few rabbits. You don't need dozens of bunnies to learn a great deal—and to have a lot of fun.

CHAPTER 8

Enjoying Your Rabbits

There's more to owning rabbits than just feeding, cleaning, and care. Take time to have fun with them, too!

Rabbits are fun. In fact, you've probably already figured that out. Owning rabbits, taking them to shows, feeding and caring for them—these are rewarding pursuits that can bring a lot of enjoyment.

But you can also have fun with your rabbits in other ways too. In this chapter, we'll discuss toys, rabbit hopping competitions, rabbit agility competitions, and house rabbits.

Fun 'n' Games

You probably wouldn't believe me if I told you I have a rabbit that demands toys, but it's absolutely true. She used to pull her water cup off of the cage wall, dump the water, and then carry the cup around her cage in her mouth. I would remove the cup, refill it, and put it back. An hour or two later, she would be carrying the cup around the cage again. Well, let's just say that it didn't take me long to replace her water cup with a "locked" version that affixed tightly to the cage wall, and to give her a toy to play with. Now, she loves her toys and plays with them regularly.

If you have a rabbit with a penchant for toys, what are the best types to choose?

Small-pet catalogs offer a wide variety of choices, and you can rest easy knowing that they are specially designed for small-animal use. You can find balls, "hay wheels," and grass mats. The grass mats are particularly interesting, as they can take the place of a resting board in your rabbit's

Grass floor mats are a natural alternative to plastic that your rabbit can munch on, if desired!

Toys won't interest all rabbits, but if you have a rabbit that enjoys playing with certain objects, you'll certainly be entertained by observing him as he plays!

cage, but since they are made of dried grass (hay), it's perfectly all right if your rabbit decides to eat it.

If you'd rather use items that you already have around the house, such as empty paper towel tubes or recycled soda cans, make sure that you choose items that don't pose any danger to your rabbits. Baby or toddler toys can make suitable toys for rabbits, as can some cat toys.

Hop To It!

Rabbit shows are undeniably fun, but if you're looking for an event with a bit more bounce, then you might want to look into rabbit agility and rabbit hopping competitions. If you're at all familiar with dog agility competitions, then you know that they offer a wide variety of obstacles for the dog to maneuver over, around, or through. Rabbit agility is essentially the same, although the obstacles are

proportionally smaller. Rabbit agility is still gaining momentum, but many rabbit enthusiasts are discovering it as a great way to interact with their rabbits and have a lot of fun at the same time.

Similar to rabbit agility, but with a slightly different twist, is rabbit hopping. Instead of an agility course, imagine a show jumping competition for horses scaled down to rabbit size. In rabbit hopping competitions, the rabbit, wearing a body harness and leash, makes its way around a course of jumps, leaping over each one. Rabbit hopping competitions are popular in Europe, particularly Scandinavia (the sport originated in Sweden), but they are just becoming known in North America.

Some rabbit breeds are not particularly well suited to agility or hopping, either due to their large size or excessive wool. However, most midsize rabbits with short coats would be suitable candidates

Rabbit agility and hopping competitions can be enjoyable for you and your rabbit, and they are quickly gaining in popularity.

for training. The exercise presents a nice diversion for your rabbit and allows the two of you to enjoy a pleasant occupation.

House Rabbits

Your rabbits are your pets, and you enjoy their company. So it's likely that you have considered the idea of having house rabbits. A house rabbit is a rabbit that is allowed to roam freely throughout your home (or at least throughout a room or two) and is kept in a hutch or cage only on occasion.

There are a number of advantages to keeping your rabbits in your home. You have the opportunity to truly enjoy your pets and their personalities, and they have the benefit of ample exercise and exploration. On the other hand, there are a fair number of disadvantages as well. Rabbits are notoriously destructive in the home, and you may find yourself dealing with chewed furniture or belongings,

droppings on the floor if a bunny isn't 100 percent litter trained, and difficulties with your other house pets. Your family dog or cat can prove to be a danger to your house rabbit, so never leave them together unsupervised. Other household dangers that can pose potential hazards to your

The first step in getting started with rabbit hopping competitions is to get your rabbit used to wearing a harness and leash.

This rabbit is hiding underneath a wicker chair. One part of rabbit-proofing your home is to eliminate hiding places, because if they are there, your bunny will undoubtedly find them.

Not so fast! This Holland Lop is attempting to expand her horizons by climbing the stairs. This is a potentially dangerous situation.

> You will have to extensively rabbit-proof your home if you decide to go the house rabbit route.

house rabbit include houseplants (these can be poisonous) and electrical cords (potentially fatal if chewed).

For these reasons, you will have to extensively rabbit-proof your home if you decide to go the house rabbit route. It's recommended that you allow your rabbit access to only one or two rooms so that you can focus on fully rabbit-proofing them. Remove any plants or electrical cords, and look around for any objects that you wouldn't want chewed. Then look around for any potential hazards: Is there

Even if you allow your rabbit to roam throughout your home, you'll still want to keep a cage available. You might want to place your rabbit in the cage when you're not at home.

House rabbits are fun because you can enjoy their company more frequently.

anything your bunny could fall off of? Are there any heavy objects that might fall on your bunny? By taking the time to fully evaluate your rabbit's future home, you'll be helping to ensure your rabbit's safety and your own peace of mind.

The final step in preparing for a house rabbit is to train him to use the litter box. This isn't actually as difficult as it might sound, since bunnies are naturally tidy creatures. You may have noticed that your rabbit has chosen a corner of his hutch that is his preferred area for relieving himself. Capitalize on this preference when you begin training him to use the litter box. Begin by placing a new litter box in that favored hutch corner. Ideally he will continue to use that corner, but he will now be relieving himself in the litter box. Once he is used to the box, you can bring it out and place it in an obvious place in your home. Rabbits are very sensitive to smell, and he will recognize his own odor on the

litter box. Don't expect him to understand immediately that the box is for his personal use, but if he makes a mistake on the floor, pick up and place the droppings in the litter box. Repeat regularly. Many bunnies will follow the scent and begin using the litter box on their own. Remember, he may continue to make a mistake from time to time, but patience is the key.

For playtime outside in an exercise pen, you might want to use a tunnel to provide shade for your rabbits.

CHAPTER 8

If there's one piece of advice that I'd like you to remember after reading this book, it would be this: enjoy your rabbits! *Shutterstock*

Glossary

6/8 breed. Any breed that has six class divisions at ARBA shows (senior buck, senior doe, intermediate buck, intermediate doe, junior buck, and junior doe). Intermediate rabbits are six to eight months old. All 6/8 breeds mature over nine pounds.

ARBA. The abbreviation of the American Rabbit Breeders Association, a national organization that recognizes forty-seven rabbit breeds and maintains registrations.

broken. A coat color pattern consisting of white intermixed with color.

buck. A male rabbit.

Certificate of Development (COD). The first step in officially developing a new breed or variety for sanction with the ARBA.

Charlie. A broken-colored rabbit that has two copies of the broken gene. Charlies exhibit improper markings for show.

conditioning. Preparing a rabbit for show; aiming for optimal body condition and fur.

coprophagy. When a rabbit ingests his own "night feces."

crown. A term commonly used in lop breeds to describe the top of the head where the ears attach.

cull. A rabbit that has been removed from its herd, typically because it does not conform to the breed standard or has a problematic health issue.

dam. A rabbit's mother.

dewlap. A flap of skin and fur under the chin of some female rabbits.

disqualification (DQ). The presence of a characteristic that is not allowed under ARBA standards, such as improperly colored toenails or malocclusion of the teeth. An animal can be disqualified from competition or disqualified from registration.

doe. A female rabbit.

dwarf. A rabbit that matures to less than four pounds.

fly back coat. A type of coat in which the fur immediately "flies back" into the original position after being pushed in the opposite direction (unlike a roll back coat).

fostering. The act of transferring young kits to a different mother, either due to an extremely large or small number of kits, or in the event of orphaned kits.

fryer. A rabbit, raised for meat, that is less than ten weeks old and weighs less than five pounds.

gestation. The length of a doe's pregnancy, usually twenty-eight to thirty-three days.

granding. Earning three legs at ARBA shows and becoming a Grand Champion.

heritage breed. A rare or endangered breed. Eleven rabbit breeds are listed on the conservation priority list of the American Livestock Breeds Conservancy.

hutch. The enclosure in which a rabbit is housed, typically consisting of a wooden frame with wire sides and floor.

junior. Any rabbit less than six months of age.

kindling. The birth and delivery of baby rabbits.

kits. Baby rabbits not yet weaned from their mother.

leg. A title earned by a rabbit for certain show wins.

litter. The baby rabbits produced at one birth by one doe.

malocclusion. Misalignment of the teeth; also known as buck teeth or wolf teeth.

meat pen. A class at county fairs and rabbit shows, consisting of an entry of three meat rabbits of the same breed and age.

mixed breed. A rabbit with ancestry that consists of two or more different breeds.

molting. The process of shedding fur; usually occurs annually for a period of a few weeks in adult rabbits. Regular brushing during the molting process is beneficial for removing excess hair and speeds the molting process.

nest box. A wooden or metal box in which a doe raises her litter of kits. The nest box is usually filled with straw or hay, wood shavings, and fur.

pedigree. Documentation of a purebred rabbit's ancestry.

posing. The proper position in which a rabbit is to be shown for exhibition. There are five posing positions, dependent upon breed.

purebred. A rabbit that is descended entirely from rabbits of one particular breed.

roll back coat. A type of coat in which the fur stays "fluffed up" when pushed in the opposite of its natural direction (unlike a fly back coat).

senior. Any rabbit over six months of age; or, in 6/8 breeds, any rabbit over eight months of age.

sire. A rabbit's father.

tattoo. A permanent mark of identification. The breeder's personal ID is located in the left ear of a rabbit; the ARBA registration number is located in the right ear.

trio. A group of three rabbits, consisting of one buck and two does, all of the same breed; intended for breeding.

Resources

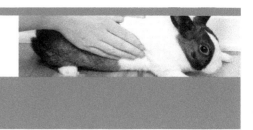

Essential Rabbit Resources

4-H. The main 4-H organization site.
http://4-h.org

American Rabbit Breeders Association.
A must-join organization for any rabbit
enthusiast. www.arba.net

Evans Software. A resource for computer
software to keep your rabbitry
organized; recommended by many
rabbit breeders.
http://evans-software.com

FFA. The main FFA organization site.
www.ffa.org

Rabbit Equipment Suppliers

Bass Equipment Company.
www.bassequipment.com

Bunny Rabbit. www.bunnyrabbit.com

Klubertanz Equipment Co., Inc.
www.klubertanz.com

KW Cages. www.kwcages.com

Rabbit Information

Rabbit Agility. Information about agility
competitions for rabbits.
www.rabbitagility.com

Rabbit Geek. Information on breeds,
lots of links, and excellent articles—
you'll have fun at this website.
www.rabbitgeek.com

Small Animal Channel. Information
on rabbit care.
www.smallanimalchannel.com

Books

American Rabbit Breeders Association.
*Official Guide Book: Raising Better
Rabbits & Cavies*. Bloomington, IL:
American Rabbit Breeders Association,
2000. This is a helpful guidebook that is
provided free of charge when you join
the ARBA.

American Rabbit Breeders Association.
Standard of Perfection 2006–2010.
Bloomington, IL: American Rabbit
Breeders Association, 2006. If you
want to be successful in raising and
showing rabbits, then you need a copy
of this book. It details the standards of
all forty-seven breeds recognized by
the ARBA.

Johnson, Samantha and Daniel Johnson.
How to Raise Rabbits. Minneapolis,
MN: Voyageur Press, 2008. With over
two hundred color photographs, this
comprehensive books details all aspects
of rabbit care, including housing,
feeding, health, rabbitry management,
colony raising, and breeding.

Johnson, Samantha. *The Field Guide to
Rabbits*. St. Paul, MN: Voyageur Press,
2008. An in-depth guide to all forty-
seven breeds recognized by the ARBA,
including color photographs of each
breed and of rabbit colors.

Index

About the Author and Photographer

uthor **Samantha Johnson** is a 4-H alumna who has been raising rabbits for more than twenty years. The author of *The Field Guide to Rabbits*, she currently keeps purebred Dutch, Holland Lop, and Netherland Dwarf rabbits. Visit her blog, www.howtoraiserabbits.blogspot.com, for more information on raising rabbits.

Photographer **Daniel Johnson** shoots all aspects of farm life as well as domestic animals. A 4-H alumnus, he enjoys helping young photographers with their projects. He is the author of the *4-H Guide to Digital Photography*, and his images appear in magazines, calendars, and greeting cards. Dan's work can be viewed at www.foxhillphoto.com.

A brother and sister team, Dan and Samantha have paired up to write and photograph several books, including *How to Raise Rabbits* and *How to Raise Horses*. They live on Fox Hill Farm outside the town of Phelps in far northern Wisconsin.

Courtesy of Daniel Johnson

Courtesy of Paulette Johnson

CPSIA information can be obtained
at www.ICGtesting.com
Printed in the USA
LVHW01s0022210817
545522LV00011B/11/P